Reshuffled

Praise for Reshuffled

There is no better way to understand the experiences of youth in foster care than to hear from those with this lived experience. This collection of essays illuminates the challenges experienced by children and youth in foster care, and it demonstrates the incredible resilience of these young adults. These powerful stories offer a message of hope for children and youth currently in foster care. By sharing their stories, the contributors also give unique insights into their experiences, which can inform the work of all those engaged in the child welfare system to improve outcomes for children and youth in foster care. These inspiring stories remind us that with the consistent support of caring adults, the future can be bright for all children and youth.

Tara Perry, CEO, National CASA/GAL
Association for Children

As a social worker and leader of a nonprofit organization that has served children and youth in foster care for over 40 years, I have learned much from many of the individuals represented in this book as their colleague, friend, and collaborative partner. *Reshuffled* is a unique look into the strength, courage, resilience, and resolve through the authentic stories from voices that need to be heard more often. I believe this book will inspire other children in foster care and all of us young and old to realize that never giving up and accepting support from others can open doors to reach dreams and overcome the struggles and traumas encountered on the journey of life.

Greg Peter, President & CEO of
United Methodist Family Services

What a privilege it is to read these essays of courage and strength written so beautifully in *Reshuffled: Real Stories of Hope and Resilience from Foster Care*. As we continue our work to improve the foster care system, especially for our older youth, may we find instruction and wisdom in the words on these pages. Thank you all for sharing your heart with us.

Melissa O'Neill, State Court Appointed Special
Advocate Program Coordinator, Virginia
Department of Criminal Justice Services

Quotes from youth in foster care

The book was so good! I really enjoyed reading it. I think this will help youth so much.

Angel, age 15

At first, I wasn't going to read the book but once I started, I couldn't stop. It was good.

Alex Sandton, age 18

Reshuffled

Real Stories of
Hope and **Resilience**
from Foster Care

TRACY GHARBO

LINDA PALMER

NEW YORK

LONDON • NASHVILLE • MELBOURNE • VANCOUVER

Reshuffled

Real Stories of Hope and Resilience from Foster Care

© 2021 Tracy Gharbo and Linda Palmer

Published in New York, New York, by Morgan James Publishing. Morgan James is a trademark of Morgan James, LLC. www.MorganJamesPublishing.com

Morgan James BOGO™

A **FREE** ebook edition is available for you or a friend with the purchase of this print book.

CLEARLY SIGN YOUR NAME ABOVE

Instructions to claim your free ebook edition:
1. Visit MorganJamesBOGO.com
2. Sign your name CLEARLY in the space above
3. Complete the form and submit a photo of this entire page
4. You or your friend can download the ebook to your preferred device

ISBN 9781631953118 paperback
ISBN 9781631953125 eBook
Library of Congress Control Number:
2020945438

Cover and Interior Design by:
Chris Treccani
www.3dogcreative.net

Morgan James is a proud partner of Habitat for Humanity Peninsula and Greater Williamsburg. Partners in building since 2006.

Get involved today! Visit
MorganJamesPublishing.com/giving-back

"I didn't grow up having role models. I grew up having people I didn't want to be like and seeing situations I'd never want to be in. Not all of us are dealt the right cards, but that does not mean you can't reshuffle the deck for a better outcome."

~ unknown

For all children in crisis who need to know
they have a voice and advocates.

Contents

"It was the best of times, it was the worst of times, it was the age of wisdom, it was the age of foolishness, it was the epoch of belief, it was the epoch of incredulity, it was the season of Light, it was the season of Darkness, it was the spring of hope, it was the winter of despair..."

Charles Dickens
A Tale of Two Cities (1859)

Foreword by Bud Ramey

In September of 2018 there were 437,283 children being served by the foster care system in the United States. Nearly one-third of these children (32 percent) were in relative homes, and nearly half (46 percent) were in non-relative foster family homes[1]. Many young people live in homes surrounded by love and support. For them, it may be the best of times.

This book is for those kids who did not live in such homes, and for those who still struggle in an imperfect foster home system. For them, it was, or is, the worst of times.

It's for foster parents who have abandoned love and empathy, marking time until their Creator calls for a long overdue bill. For them, it will be the worst of times.

Reshuffled is also for members of the foster parent community. For people who love a foster child. For friends of foster children. For ministers to foster kids. For social workers who wake up in the

---

1   Foster Care Statistics 2018 Children's Bureau www.childwelfare.gov

morning thinking about their kids in foster care. It's for those who have survived, aged out, and moved on, still carrying the baggage.

Within this book, you will find inspirational messages from people who have experienced the foster care system.

Some stories may bring you to tears of joy.

Some will bring tears of sadness and disbelief.

Either way, *Reshuffled* was not created to disparage a system, which though imperfect, is the only option for hundreds of thousands of youth in America. If our nation's leaders gain insight from these stories, perhaps some of the holes in the fabric could be mended.

First, one must identify and name the problem. Then solutions will appear.

We will leave the naming of the problem up to you, dear reader.

And bless you for caring enough to see what these former foster kids have to say.

Preface
About Foster Care

In the enlightening Signature Report of the Casey Family Programs in 2019 "On the Pathway of Hope," we learn that one in eight children will experience abuse or neglect by the time they are eighteen years old.

The term *foster care* evokes emotions in everyone.

For many, it brings a flashback of memories instantaneously.

If you have known a child in foster care, or if you have been in foster care, those memories are permanent, powerful, life changing.

There is power in understanding these feelings, in sharing ways of coping with the many emotional and physical challenges of not having a full complement of birth parents.

For those of us involved in the delivery of foster care, as foster care parents, as members of the judicial system, as mental health advocates and caregivers, there is great wisdom to be learned from the testimonies presented in *Reshuffled.*

Because here, our foster care veterans open their hearts and let us in. We have attempted to retain much of their personality and speaking style in the way we have presented their stories. Each account is true and affirmed as remembered by the contributor. Our hope is that you will hear their voices in your head as you read each one.

Thousands of young people are thriving in foster homes with loving foster parents. Yet the system is far from perfect. For those who have seen struggle, we are permitted, but for a moment, to see what their darkness looked like; to see how they found a light to help guide them through that abyss.

Foster care is a system in which a minor is placed into a ward, group home (residential childcare community, treatment center, etc.), or private home of a state-certified caregiver, referred to as a "foster parent" or with a family member approved by the state.

The placement of the child is usually arranged through the government or a social service agency. The institution, group home or foster parent is compensated for expenses unless with a family member. (Yet that is changing to help those who care for family members.)

The State, via the family court and child protective services agency, stand *in loco parentis* to the minor, making legal decisions while the foster parent is responsible for the day-to-day care of the minor.

Most kinship care is done informally, without the involvement of a court or public organization. However, in the U.S., formal kinship care is increasingly common. In 2012, a quarter of all children in formal foster care were placed with relatives instead of being placed into the system.

Children may enter foster care voluntarily or involuntarily. Voluntary placement may occur when a biological parent or lawful guardian is unable to care for a child. Involuntary placement occurs when a child is removed from their biological parent or lawful guardian due to the risk or actual occurrence of physical or psychological harm. The literature reveals that in the US, most children enter foster care due to neglect.

In the US, foster care started as a result of the efforts of Charles Loring Brace. In 1853, some 30,000 homeless or neglected children lived in the New York City streets and slums. Brace believed the children would do best with a Christian farm family. He did this to save them from a lifetime of suffering. He sent these children to families by train, which gave the name The Orphan Train Movement.

Jelani Freeman
Foster Care Experiences
Are Not All the Same

In November 2017, I spoke at the College of William & Mary about my experiences growing up and aging out of the foster care system. I told my audience how at age eight, I waited unrewarded for my mentally ill mother to return home to me.

Six different foster homes over a ten-year period

How my father was in prison and could not take me in. I traveled to six different foster homes over a ten-year period with only garbage bags to carry my personal items from one unfamiliar home to the next. Later in life, I beat the odds and graduated from college only to be reminded of my aloneness once again seeing everyone around me surrounded by family and loved ones sharing that special day. In some ways, my story is like many children in foster care, but I know everyone's journey is unique and should be treated that way.

After that talk at William & Mary, two ladies and their tag-along husbands came up to speak with me. They were CASA (Court Appointed Special Advocates for Neglected & Abused Children), and they wanted to encourage me to keep telling my story for other children to hear. These women wanted me to write a book or a collection of essays. It wasn't something I was ready to take on, but they did. I am collaborating on this project for you on their behalf and on the behalf of all the adults in the system who want to help foster children; CASA, mentors, social workers, Guardian Ad Litem (GALs), counselors and teachers.

I was asked to help write an essay that would give you a positive message of hope to encourage resilience and form a blueprint for a successful life. Full disclosure: I am a CASA too. Being a CASA has been extremely rewarding. The first thing I usually do is share a bit of my history. I did go through foster care and I did age out of the system. I will clarify that I'm not sharing it to demonstrate that I know exactly what you're going through because I don't. I think everybody's journey and story is different but, there are some things that I have experienced that may be familiar to you, and maybe I'm able to lend advice or consolation from that perspective.

My story is not one of abuse. My mother was mentally unable to care for me. She loved and nurtured me as a child, and my development benefited from that caring. I, like many foster children, loved my mother. Looking back as an adult, I can appreciate that she tried her best. I ended up in foster homes and group homes until aging out and moving on to college. I experienced foster parents who didn't speak to me or left me out of family trips. It was made clear I was "other" than family. My experience was not one of warmth or encouragement.

Keep an open mind

I think it's important that we understand that people's foster care experiences aren't always the same. I recognize with me and the people that were in my life, especially early on, it definitely took a lot of effort to reach me because it's not easy to work with teens and some of the issues they face. I think for teens, I would encourage you to keep an open mind. Although I didn't really recognize it at the time, I just didn't see the point in a lot of things. I was discouraged by my situation in life, and that sort of rubbed off on my attitude about most things: school, working with mentors and different things.

Luckily, what happened for me was that I was put in a program with a mentor which included an after-school job. It was something that pulled me up because I could earn some extra money. I would say I was very short sighted and didn't realize it was setting me up for much more in the long term. I was paired with someone who was going to help me get into college and be there with me throughout college, graduate school, law school and various other life events. I was also fortunate in that I basically had one social worker throughout my ten-year experience. Looking back, I realize that stability played out in my favor.

It is hard sometimes when you're younger to think about the long term and what steps you need to take to get where you want to go. You have to realize that you can't do it alone, that you'll need, in some capacity or another, people along the way to help you. I've been in Washington D.C. for 15 years now, so all the jobs I've had, I have stayed in touch with the people I worked with and with my bosses. This has opened a ton of doors where I can not only get references from them, but they'll also let me know about different opportunities for my next steps in my career and life.

My mentor was very consistent. She was consistent in her belief in me and the message of the importance of hard work and education. She let me know that she cared, and she wanted the best for me. I was skeptical, but I think there was a switch where I said, okay, maybe she is serious and maybe she really wants to help me. I think I looked at going off to college as our big thing, our big project together. I really hadn't considered it that much before having my mentor.

I was already in 11th grade when I met her, and I was behind academically. She helped pay for some SAT classes for me but even with that, I just didn't have the vision of going to school for four years. Four years just seemed like such a long time. I think she helped me understand that you want to get this education because it will help put you in a better position in life. That stuck with me, but then I think I also just wanted to get out of foster care and go live somewhere else.

Afraid of *no* answers

I think throughout all that time, she was good at keeping me focused on the long term, which is hard for a teenager.

The short term is such a strong focus like the girl you like in high school or the basketball team you're on and that's your whole world. Sometimes her consistency was like a broken record. But she really impressed upon me that there's going to be so much more after high school that you need to really set yourself up for and prepare for it. I'm thankful that she kept hammering that home because I think it worked, and now I see other people I knew growing up who have those regrets about not going to college or trade school.

She never left my side, even when I got expelled from school my senior year. I think there were maybe two months to go and I had already been accepted into college, a couple of colleges, but with the expulsion, they were going to make me come to school the following year, so I wouldn't have been able to finish that spring. We had to go down to the school board and appeal and do all this extra stuff, and she was there with me every step of the way.

Luckily, we successfully appealed it and I got to finish my exams. I didn't get to go to graduation, but I was just happy to be done and able to go on to college. Looking back at it now, I could see how disheartening that could have been for her. It didn't really phase her. She just asked, "What do we have to do to get you to graduate?" She stuck with me through ups and downs and then throughout college.

I give her credit too because the thing is, she has a daughter the same age as me. We went to college and graduated at the same time. So, at times it was difficult for her to make me a priority. I understood she had a daughter who came first, but she always found a way to make sure I knew that I mattered too. I always give the caveat that, even though at my graduation, there was really no one there for me.

I know if she could have been there, she would have been. She did attend my law school graduation with a dozen other supporters which was a tremendously joyful day. She was definitely there to encourage and help me as much as she could. And at times I listened and times I didn't. However, even now to this day, she's retired and she's a little less active, but I still call her for council.

I've always made the calculation that if you're willing to help yourself, you'll get a lot of people who are interested in helping you also. I've always seen that if I am working towards something it makes people gravitate to be at my side and want me to succeed. Many people fail to ask for help, whether it's their pride or they're afraid of no answers. I really can't explain it except to say that I've always had pretty good people in my corner.

Even when I've thought they weren't. I remember I had one professor that I had a lot in college. I always thought she really didn't like me. Then I found myself boxed in because I needed a reference from a professor for grad school and since I had taken a bunch of classes with her, I had to suck it up and ask her.

We had a conversation and she agreed to write a reference for me. I was honest with her and said I always thought, by the way she treated me, that she didn't like me, and she said it wasn't that at all. She thought I had much more potential than I was using and that's why she was always so hard on me. Since that time, we've stayed in contact and she's been a good support.

I think approaching people with sincerity and genuine honesty has helped me.

There are really only two things that can happen when you reach out to people: they can either say yes or they can say no, and you don't know until you ask. But I really do think a big thing is I've always wanted to demonstrate that I was willing to sacrifice and help myself before I went and asked for any help. I always thought that was a pretty good selling point to say, "Hey, I've done this, this, and this and I just need this much more help if you could help me."

I think people are impressed that you've taken different steps to do what you needed to do, and it makes them want to help you.

I think the one thing that I would say, and to be honest I didn't always have, and that is to believe in yourself and your talents. It is extremely, extremely important. Having a certain amount of confidence in what you do is pretty key and really the start of anything you want to do. I think many times throughout my childhood, I didn't have confidence. There are things that I shied away from, things that I didn't jump into because I just didn't know if I could do it.

I would say to you—wherever you get it from—have that confidence and belief in yourself because before anybody else can believe in you, you have to believe in yourself. It's life, whether you fail or succeed, you never want to look back and say, "you didn't even try."

I think about that for myself and I think about that for other young people I encounter, especially from the foster care system because it's tough. I think where some other young people may get that encouragement and building up of their self-esteem from their parents and the people around them, sometimes foster children must find it within themselves or go look for it in other places. Otherwise, you're selling yourself short from the beginning.

My big advice to young people; believe in yourselves, be confident and dream big. I'd never thought about being a lawyer until I was a full-grown adult. I had known other lawyers but never thought that I could do it until I had that exposure. I started to understand it is not as hard as I thought it was. Even without that, I wish I would've had the confidence to know that it would have been within my reach if that's what I really wanted to do.

Take advice from the people who want the best for you and look to the long term.

Believe in yourself, be confident, and dream big.

Sometimes it takes saying it over and over again before finally, finally you hear it.

Jelani Freeman is a community leader, attorney, and motivational speaker who has dedicated his life to serving children. His commitment to kids grew from his time in multiple foster homes, shelters, group homes and juvenile facilities. Jelani Freeman entered the foster care system in Rochester, New York at the age of 8, when his mother was no longer able to care for him, and he spent most of his youth in foster care before he aged out of the system.

Driven by his determination to be a voice for voiceless children, Jelani has worked for multiple agencies that serve youth, including the D.C. Department of Youth Rehabilitation Services, where he served as the architect of many of the Department's positive youth development programs. Jelani has spent his career working in government, starting with a Senate internship for Hillary Clinton in 2003, which propelled him to speak about his personal story at the July 2016 Democratic National Convention.

Jelani earned a law degree from Howard University School of Law in Washington D.C. in 2010. He also has a bachelor's degree in Political Science and History from State University of New York (SUNY) Buffalo and a Master's degree in History from American University in Washington D.C. Currently, he works as an Appellate Attorney for the Department of Veterans Affairs. He also serves as a Court Appointed Special Advocate (CASA) in D.C. and sits on the Boards of the Center for Adoption Support and Education (CASE) and the D.C. Office of Employee Appeals (OEA).

Gia Smith

Too Good to Be True:
Life After Hurricane Katrina

I was fifteen years old when I went through Hurricane Katrina.

Growing up in New Orleans is a completely different environment and culture than anywhere else. It was all I had ever experienced, so it was my normal. I didn't see anything wrong with my life. It is only looking back now, that I realize that no child should be put through the abuse and neglect I experienced.

I had heard about the hurricane coming, but you just grow up with that. We didn't take it seriously. I came home one day, and my family had packed up the house and left. Everything was gone. I was by myself.

I went to my friend's where we tried to prepare, but we didn't think it would be as bad as it was. We heard a loud boom, like a bomb going off. The levees had broken, and the water was rushing in. The rest of the hurricane is a blur. We rode it out. The worst was after the hurricane passed; dead bodies, dead animals, washed away homes, and no running water or electricity. We had life jackets and military packet food, but we had to figure an escape route to safety.

I was put on a bus with my friend, her mom, and their other kids. I didn't have a choice where I was going. My friend's mom was growing frustrated with an extra child to worry about, so she went to a police station. The police actually brought me to my mom who was in Texas. She asked the police what she had to do legally to drop me off and be done with me. She didn't want to be charged with neglect.

The police officer put me in his car, and he had a conversation with me. He cried. He couldn't believe what he was seeing, but I was used to that sort of stuff.

The policeman took me to a safe place. I think it was a transitional home for girls. Mentally, I'm feeling like it's my fault, not my mom's. I told the staff there that I thought I might be pregnant. I took three pregnancy tests that all came back negative.

They thought I was making it up for attention. They convinced me I wasn't pregnant. I was put in a temporary foster home where I had to have a physical. That was when the doctor said, "We have an issue" and told me and my foster mom that I was pregnant.

My foster mom said her home was a temporary home, she didn't take babies, and I wouldn't be going back there. Not only that, but I was admitted to the hospital right away, because I was in labor. The baby was four months and one week at that point. I stayed on bedrest for two months. My baby wasn't due until

Halloween, but I had him on July 23rd at twenty-four weeks. He weighed one pound, three ounces.

I begged to stay in my foster home. It was my first introduction to a lifestyle different from the one I knew in New Orleans. I was comfortable and felt safe. They let me stay for three months while my baby, Chaz, was in the hospital, and then I went to live with the Mersbergers in a new foster home. At the time, I thought these people just wanted my baby.

They were so concerned about his safety and his living conditions. Basically, that is where he was going to go whether I was on board or not. They were licensed for special disability. I just thought it was a negative situation, but I wanted to be with him, and so when they offered me the opportunity to come along, I took it reluctantly.

I didn't think it was going to be a good situation.

And then I moved in. I moved in before Chaz came home from the hospital, and *I loved it!* They were a family. They were togetherness. They ate at the table. They talked about life. I don't know, just everything was 100% different from what I was used to, but *I loved it.* I liked it. I wanted more. I didn't want to leave. I was excited about my baby coming home there.

This couldn't be real

At the same time, in that first year, I just kept thinking there had to be a scam behind it. There must be something they are getting out of it. They couldn't really love me and my child. This couldn't be real. There were many times I would say, what do you care? Why am I here? What are you getting out of it?

My foster dad (really both of them) invested a lot of time and love in me. He would ask what was going on in my mind. A therapist would come to the house a couple of times a week and I was very vocal about what I was feeling. I'd say, "I like this, but I feel like there's just something fishy behind it. It is too good to be true."

I was excelling at high school when this realization hit me. I was a person with all of these possibilities. I can succeed and do things in life, but I also had all these experiences; abuse, abandonment, that other kids hadn't had. That was hard. I had a lot to process. I had a lot of therapy. I was angry and frustrated. I talked a lot. I wanted to reach out to my mom and have a relationship with her.

It was very confusing. When I learned she had had her parental rights terminated completely, it was confirmation that this person is really not for me. I had had a baby and she never responded to anything. My foster parents had found my grandparents, and I had started a relationship with them.

Baby Chaz needed a lot of care. My foster mom was very proactive getting him lots of services every week. But I knew he would have issues because of bleeding in his brain. At the same time, I was still having issues with anger, aggression, and confusion on a daily basis.

Over time, seeing the relationship my adult foster siblings had with the Mersbergers helped me a lot. When they would come back home and visit, it was just a family unit. It wasn't like, this is a foster home situation. No one was treated differently. I could see there was no difference if you were adopted, foster, or biological. You were just home.

I think one of the things that stood out for me was when some of my siblings would have issues and things going on in their lives, they were never treated differently. No matter the issue, they were still trusted. I judged them, but the Mersbergers didn't. They were never watched and treated like criminals. They were loved and they felt home. They were with Nana and Poppy.

Then, they started discussing college, like it could be a reality. It became something I could do!

For the rest of high school, I had a great pregnancy counselor. She would get all the pregnant and teen moms throughout the school, and we would have events. She would arrange to pick us up with our kids to go to church every single Wednesday night. We were family and when I would see cousins and siblings at school, it was a natural thing. There wasn't any bias.

I loved school. Growing up, my mom didn't care about education. It wasn't a priority for her. In spite of that, I excelled at school in New Orleans. I was in ROTC and choir, but my mom never showed up, paid any fees, or took any interest in the things I was doing for myself. I just got used to trying things and not having them work out. Now in Dallas, I became involved in soccer and traveled with the team. My family supported me. We even began looking at colleges together.

One thing that bothered me in the beginning was the question, *what are you going to do with your life?*

I didn't want to think about it.

I didn't want to write stuff down. But once I was pushed to do it, I saw that I loved going to school, learning, and setting goals. The rest is history.

I worked different jobs and my senior year in high school, I was promoted to night assistant manager at QuikTrip. The Mersbergers helped me get my own home just before I graduated. Chaz was in a good daycare/school and receiving a lot of therapy. My family helped me with him while I worked or went to school. Chaz loved sleeping in Nana's bed. I started college that fall at Tarrant County College, 4.0 my first year!

But I dropped out. I was comfortable. I had friends and a good relationship with the Mersbergers. I was making good money for my age. I was providing for me and Chaz. But my chemistry course had discouraged me. I worked hard with tutors, but I had to take it twice. My baby sister, Maddy, challenged me. She was a freshman in high school, living with the Mersbergers and she said, "You need to think about what you want to do with your life. By the time I'm a senior, you need to have a plan going."

That's my baby sister talking to me!

It hit home, so I said to myself, *"Okay, I'll do it."* I went back and re-enrolled. I graduated with an associate degree in arts and psychology. Then I transferred and graduated from the University of North Texas with a Bachelor of Arts and Science, concentrating in science rehabilitation, social work, and behavioral analysis. I specialize in disabilities of all kinds, including autism. I earned a place on the Dean's List and the President's List.

Foster care is the best thing that ever happened to me. My advice is for the people in a position to help. Here it is.

Understand how much diversity, environment, and culture play a part. Even though a child may have been molested or abused, it is normal to them. So, when someone comes in and wants to change everything, a child cannot see life in that light.

When a child's control is taken away, too often they are not given a full understanding of what is happening. The adults with all the control need to understand that a child will feel more comfortable in a bad situation they know, than in a new one they don't know. Children love their parents no matter what.

To the children in foster care, be open to change.

Try to see the good in people.

It's hard to see the good in people and still not question. Be open to trust and love. Be open to someone who wants to be in your life. You might look back and feel guilty about doing better. It's okay to accept something better.

Today, Gia is the proud parent of Chaz, a highly intelligent, high functioning teenager on the autism spectrum. Gia contributed to this book while on bed rest as she awaited the birth of her second child. A healthy Ocean Shay Smith arrived at thirty-five weeks, weighing six pounds fourteen ounces.

She is currently employed at Allied Universal and also finds time to mentor teens.

Delegate David Reid
From There to Here:
A Life Reset

When you start running for office, people want to know who you are and how you got to this point. I never thought to share my story until now because this is just who I am, but as I get older and look back, I can see there were decision points and forks in the road.

Have you ever been called to the Principal's office?

It is a very long walk

I was in the fourth grade, about ten years old, in Rockbridge County, Virginia when I was called to the office. But instead of being in trouble, they informed me that they collected clothes for the poor children in my school and here was my box of clothes. That was the first time I really knew I was poor. We lived in a four-room house, not four bedrooms, a four-room house with an outhouse.

We actually never went hungry because we ate a lot of oatmeal, brown beans, fried bologna, hog jowl, and potatoes. My dad would heat bricks in a wood stove to put in our beds to keep us warm at night. It was 1972, and my dad made about $3,000 a year to take care of five kids because my mother had left us when I was six years old.

My dad made the decision that he couldn't take care of us anymore, so he took us to the Methodist Children's Home in Richmond, Virginia where we were divided up by age and gender to live in different cottages. How self-aware are you really when you are ten years old? I don't know, but I remember being in a very large cottage with a bunch of other boys who were my age and I was aware enough to know that I had an indoor bathroom and hot and cold running water.

I got different meals every day. So, it was not a bad thing for me. My dad got a job at the Children's Home, and we would eat dinner with him. Meals added another weird family dynamic because he was no longer responsible for our day to day care, feeding, or discipline.

At the Children's Home, we went to the Methodist Church every Sunday and to public school during the week. Like many children in a new school system, I was picked on. Looking back on that time, I recognize that I had two choices – either to become negative by the abuse or let it help me become empathetic and more understanding of how others cope who are facing similar situations.

I chose the second path, to try to understand.

One of the things that helped me finally become more accepted in the years between fifth and eighth grade was sports. I was able to help the team, so I became one of the guys. Sports were an equalizer. But I also began skipping school and getting in fights, so John Gregory, the assistant administrator at the Children's Home, and my dad decided I needed more structure and they sent me to Randolph-Macon Academy for my freshman and sophomore years of high school.

Institutions

I went to school at an institution and on holidays came home to another institution.

The next year, John Gregory, my foster dad, got a job at another children's home in Tahlequah, Oklahoma. He and his wife, Jean, decided to foster/adopt me and one of my brothers, Mark.

I should mention my other siblings. My oldest sister Priscilla is very smart but effectively became the surrogate mother when my mom left. As expected of any high school teenager, this was not to her liking, and she dropped out of high school and got married the last semester before graduating.

My next oldest sister, Mary, went to the Children's Home, and they let her stay past the usual eighteen years old so she could attend business school and become a legal secretary. She later tapped into her artistic gifts, and she and her husband started their own internet business which has now grown to five employees, including my sister, Priscilla.

Daniel, my first youngest brother, is thirteen months younger than me. The Gregorys did not think they would find the services Daniel needed in Oklahoma, so he was not adopted. Daniel now has his own taxicab company in the Roanoke-Salem area.

Mark and I went to Oklahoma with the Gregorys to finish high school. It was a very awkward time because when you move to a new high school, especially mid-high school cycle, not just during the middle part of the year, you don't know anyone. Everybody else has been there forever. To add to that, for the past two years, I had been told every day what to wear, how to cut my hair, and where I was supposed to be every minute of every day.

Suddenly, I'm in public school and what do I wear?

What are the right clothes?

What's my hair supposed to look like?

How do I fit in?

All of the travails that go along with being in high school are amplified when you are brand new. I had played football at Randolph-Macon Academy, and I was pretty good. I wanted to try out at Tahlequah, but I hadn't been there for the first few years of high school, and I wasn't good enough to just come in and earn a spot on the team.

On the other hand, my brother, Mark, ended up being the star football player. He married his high school sweetheart and went to Okmulgee Technical Institute. He's still in Oklahoma, has two grown daughters, and has done very well for himself. His church is very important in his life, and occasionally they will make mission trips to Africa.

As I think about the Gregorys, my foster and adoptive parents who I still keep in touch with today, I understand that they opened their home and their hearts to me and my brother. They really wanted us to succeed. Foster kids can be disruptive to established family units. The Gregorys did not have children.

Maybe we filled a gap for them. Maybe they wanted to give back, but they invited us in and made accommodations for us. We needed to be appreciative of that. There's something about the human spirit that makes room in our hearts for that second child and that third child. There's something in the human spirit for those folks who want to foster and adopt children, and they are doing it out of love, and they want their adopted or fostered child to succeed just as much as if they were their birth parents.

No one in my family had ever gone to college, ever, not even back to the 1700s. I hadn't thought about going to college. It had never occurred to me because I had not really been exposed to the idea. When you grow up where I grew up, college isn't generally considered an option. After high school graduation, folks kept asking me, "what are you going to do in the fall? Where are you going to college?"

So, I was like "Well, I'm going to Northeastern Oklahoma State University," which is, no kidding, literally on the other side of town. I applied and got accepted. I went with a friend I had met in high school, John deSteiguer. Now I've been in the community for two years and I'm going to college, brand new, and I have an opportunity to, in some respects, do a reset of who I am and how I want to move forward.

I can choose what groups I want to participate in and which ones I don't want to participate in, and I'm not concerned about the high school environment. For me, life became much more of a meritocracy because if you do well, you will succeed.

My major was political science with minors in history and economics. I became very active in three groups that would influence the rest of my life: Student Senate, Model United Nations (MUN), and the Oklahoma Intercollegiate Legislature (OIL). The Oklahoma Intercollegiate Legislature is a version of the Virginia General Assembly, except that it is made up of college students. I was elected Governor of the Oklahoma Intercollegiate Legislature. John became Speaker of the House. Here we were, from this little, tiny school in the northeastern part of the state and we've got the most senior positions in the legislature as opposed to the big schools, Oklahoma University and Oklahoma State.

I had gone from being an awkward junior in high school to a person having all these opportunities. It didn't happen by accident. It was always a lot of hard work. I remember thinking my junior year of college, when I was 21, that I'm on the cusp of graduating and if I look back to the last ten years of my life, when I was 11 years old, I was just arriving at the children's home after living in poverty.

Now I'm on the verge of becoming the first person in my family to earn a college degree. I'm living the American Dream. I decided that I owed something back to my country. That's when I sought out and joined the Navy Reserves to become a Naval Intelligence Officer, which would give me top secret security clearance.

I couldn't have planned this out. I was just doing the very best job I could at whatever job I had been given to do and then took advantage of the opportunities that presented themselves.

There were setbacks along the way. I got married, the first time, in my junior year of college. I was much too young, but we were married for five years. When my ex-wife told me she no longer wanted to be married, it was devastating.

I thought I was over the scars of having my mother leave, but now old wounds that I had been carrying with me were opened up again. Yet, I was determined that I wasn't going to let it get me down.

Another setback occurred after finishing college. I wanted to go to Capitol Hill in D.C., but I was only able to get a temporary job through the end of the election. I literally had to take stuff off my resume so I didn't look overqualified to get my first job as a bank teller. I'm thinking to myself, I have just gone to college, done all these great things, and now I'm only making $11,000 a year.

Regardless of what modern time period you're talking about, that's not a lot of money. Initially, I think what drove me so hard was a fear of failure. I knew where I had come from and I was probably only one job away from being back there. That fear of failure drove me to work harder and do a very good job at everything I tried. After a long time you do finally get beyond that fear and develop as an adult, but in the beginning, that's what drove me.

One job leads to another

My first long-term job out of college was as a bank teller and as time began to unfold, one job led to another. Because I had some public speaking experience from college extracurricular activities, the bank asked me to be one of their trainers. Then because I had security clearance through the Navy Reserve, I was given the opportunity to become a computer trainer at the National Reconnaissance Office.

Having done training, that led to a job teaching "Intro to Computing" and "Intro to Networking" at Strayer University. Later, since I had banking experience, I was asked to become a financial program manager for a subsidiary of British Telecom (BT). I had always had an interest in international affairs and always wanted to travel, and this opportunity finally presented itself while I was working for BT and later AT&T.

Today, as the Democratic Representative from the 32nd District to the Virginia General Assembly, I have come full circle from my experiences in college. As you can see, it was not a straight path.

I have always said to my daughters, "Do the very best job in whatever job you've been asked to do, and people will recognize it."

Now here I am in the Virginia General Assembly. When in Richmond, my wife and I attend the same Methodist church I frequented while at the Children's Home so many years ago. One

Sunday, we went to the early service. While waiting for the service to begin, four or five children came in and sat down behind us. I figured they were with the Children's Home, now called United Methodist Family Services.

I introduced myself and told them, "I have been where you are."

I kind of have an idea of how their lives could lay out before them.

I feel like if I can do it, then anybody can do it. I invited them to come to the Virginia State Capitol. When I spotted them up in the gallery, I asked them to stand and be recognized. I also asked some other delegates who had been adopted to stand. I talked about getting from *there to here* and the fact that anybody can do it.

The children wrote some really nice follow-up letters, but one that really stuck with me wrote, "I didn't think that I was going to amount to anything, and now I feel like I can do anything." That's awesome. Yeah, that's really awesome.

I would never want to wish my childhood on anyone, but it did make me who I am today and I'm comfortable with who I am today, and so that's the positive take-away.

Was it hard along the way?

Yes.

Was it difficult?

Was it sometimes very painful and very hurtful?

Yes, but again, had my mother not left, had my dad not decided to take us to the Children's Home, I'd probably still be in Rockbridge County. I probably never would have gone to college and probably never gotten into the Navy.

I can look back on it now and say, *I wouldn't want to wish this on you, but it made me who I am right now.*

Today, I usually find that I am the most optimistic person in a room and I really do truly believe that you can achieve anything. I choose to take away the positive from my experiences.

David A. Reid is the Democratic Representative to the Virginia House of Delegates, one of two governing bodies in the Virginia General Assembly.

He is a Retired United States Navy Commander.

Raeshawn Smith
Believe in the People
Who Love You

grew up in Alexandria, Virginia with my mom. My dad was in and out of prison, so he really wasn't in the picture then. My mom had a really bad drug problem.

She abused drugs a lot and also physically abused us because when you're on that stuff, you are not yourself.

But she was my mother and I thought it was normal. There were times when I got pretty hurt. Me and my three siblings would be left in the house for days at a time while she was binging. My older brother, who was about nine, had to be the man of the house.

He would make us sandwiches and do whatever was needed to keep food in our bellies. Eventually, social services got a whiff of what was going on.

One day, I came home from school and everything was kind of going haywire. I was seven and didn't understand what was happening. Everyone was crying, even my one-year-old little brother. There were these strange people in the house, and they took us.

I remember it like it was yesterday.

They put us into this car, and I could see my mom crying in the back yard as we drove off. That's a very vivid memory for me. We didn't know where we were going or for how long. It wound up being three years.

Me and my older brother were separated from our younger siblings. They were in one foster home for the whole duration. They were with the Murphys, great people who are still our friends to this day.

But me and my older brother, we bounced around to seven different houses throughout that time span. I think the longest we were in one home was nine months. We had to keep switching schools, which was really annoying and unstable. But what could we do about it?

We were really young and didn't have any control. As time went along, I was gathering an understanding of why we were in this predicament. I didn't cope very well without my siblings, especially my sister. We are really close in age and physical appearance. People mistake us for twins all the time. We have a link. So, I was very distraught being away from them.

I would cry at night because I couldn't see them.

We only visited our siblings about once a month. Eventually, we got to visit my dad and my siblings once a week. But it wasn't enough. I wanted to see them every day. I wanted to see my mom every day. It was really sad. While my mom was in rehab, she would write us letters telling us she loved us and how sorry she was. They were long letters in her beautiful handwriting.

When my dad got out of prison, he had found out we were in foster care and started the process to try and get us.

But as a convicted felon, he had to do a lot to prove that he was a fit parent. We started living with my dad when I was ten years old, but even that wasn't easy because it was hard for my dad to get a job.

A lot of times we didn't have hot water or lights or both. During that time, we would have to go to a family friend's house for a month or two just so we could get back on our feet. We were never really comfortable. There is one thing that can never be denied of my parents. They love their kids to death. My mom, she's obviously made mistakes, but when it comes down to it, my mom and dad love their kids. You can't question that.

I'm so grateful to have parents that love their children so much because, as rough as it was for me growing up, there are kids out there in worse situations who are abandoned and unloved. I feel lucky.

A lot of times I looked at my mom's drug addiction and thought you love drugs more than you love your kids. But as I got older, I understood that that stuff consumes you. My mom could never really kick the habit, even to this day. It's called addiction for a reason. It's a sickness. I will never touch a drug ever in my life.

You can 100 percent guarantee it.

There are drugs all around me now, but as soon as someone tries to offer me any, I'm like, *no, I'm good.* That's that. I've even been in situations or relationships with girls that start messing with certain things and I'm, *alright we're done.* I can't do that because it literally tore my family apart. This is a deal breaker for me.

In fact, none of my nine siblings use drugs. I think that is a very clear reflection of what we went through.

My dad went to prison for distributing drugs, and my mom used drugs, which is a terrible, terrible mix. My dad basically told us, learn from my mistakes. Do not do this because it is a dead-end street. Countless times he said, *I don't care how hard things get mentally, financially, don't do it. It's not worth it. Look how hard it is for me to get a job. I hate myself for it and I'm struggling all the time. Drugs are just never the answer.*

He was a good role model and a really fair disciplinarian. He never put his hands on us. He taught us right from wrong and would explain why. He was a really good father.

While we were still in foster care, a driver took us back and forth to meet up with our dad and siblings, and he became so much more than a driver to us. If we had extra time, he would take us to places like Chuck E. Cheese and things like that. I think he was Middle Eastern, and he would tell us we were great kids. We wound up really loving that guy. He would say, *I know you guys are going through some stuff, but it's all going to be okay. Just stay in school, keep your head up.* It was always positive advice. He was not officially a mentor, but he acted like one.

My mom couldn't sign us up for organized sports. But me and my brother and sister were always outside playing anything we could with the other kids in the neighborhood because we knew at home, it wasn't right.

Anytime my mom started acting kind of funny, we knew, okay, let's go outside. It was a big way to get away from all the nonsense. It carried over through my foster care years. We stayed outside and we stayed active.

When we got to live with my dad, one of the first things he did was sign us up for organized sports. He played sports when he was growing up and that's kind of what dads do anyway. The first time I played in the 75-pound youth football league, I was an offensive lineman, but I didn't care, I was playing. Sports became a huge part of my life.

I was in the fourth grade, and my dad was trying really hard, but things were crazy. He was working so many hours. There were times he would pick us up from the babysitter at 2:00 a.m. or we had to walk from one babysitter's house to another's.

So, I didn't have a real solid reason why this book I was supposed to make for Ms. Molter, my teacher, wasn't on time. I tried to explain why I couldn't get it done. She gave me an extra week and when I did turn it in, it was a positive message about why you shouldn't join gangs and I had all the details about gangs.

I think that book prompted her to ask if everything was alright at home. I told her not really. She and the counselor talked to my dad, and he told them he was trying but it was hard with four kids and lots of long hours working. After that, a lot of times I would end up staying after school and Ms. Molter would help me. It made things much easier. She was one of my best teachers. She had a great sense of humor and was very charismatic. She was there to help me.

I wanted something better

It wasn't very pleasant growing up, but I have a mind over matter sort of mentality. I lived in a rough area. There weren't many opportunities or resources, so a lot of kids I grew up with wound up flunking out and selling drugs, not really making a good life for themselves. But I saw that, and I saw what that had to offer, and I wasn't trying to do that with my life. I wanted something better.

I told myself I was going to stay in school and focus because if you focus on academics, you're able to get into college and when you're able to get into college, it opens doors for you to get good jobs.

I wanted to be the kind of guy that stood out; I always wanted to be the best. I always hated when I got a B or a C.

I wanted A's.

The funny thing about self-motivation is that it's intrinsic. I felt a bunch of satisfaction always getting good grades. I've always been super diligent and meticulous. Some people say I'm a perfectionist. I don't know where I get that from. It's just the way I am, but it wound up working for me. It doesn't matter how miniscule or grand it is. I do things to the best of my ability. I always apply myself.

What I would like to tell a kid going through what I went through is that there is a silver lining.

There's a light at the end of the tunnel and even though things may be rough right now, you're going to get through it. I'm a prime example. I thought it was never going to end. I didn't know when I was going to get out of foster care, when I was going to start living with my mom or my dad. But it finally did happen.

You really have to believe in the people who love you.

Regardless of what you're going through, there are always going to be people who love you. There are always going to be people who are willing to extend a hand and help whether they're your relatives or not. It's important to use those resources. I think that is what I did. Using people like Ms. Molter and my driver. They really helped me see that life is not garbage.

There are positives. You can do something with your life regardless of what disadvantages you're given. Just stay the course and believe in yourself. Believe in everyone that believes in you and you can really make something out of yourself.

Ironically, I think what I went through made me a better person because I was able to see that the world is not all peachy and creamy.

It taught me not to look down on anyone.

When you're driving down the street past houses, you never know what's going on inside each house. So, when you meet someone, it's important not to judge them because you don't know what they are going through. I tend to give people the benefit of the doubt because I know what I went through. Some people look down on people who don't have as much money or two parents like they do.

I was teased when I was younger for having holes in my shoes and messed up clothes. It made me feel terrible and I decided I was never going to be that guy. I'm never going to be a bully. I'm never going to look down on someone because of what they're wearing or how they look or what their living situation is.

It's so ugly, so I try to be a good person to everybody.

I see the world for what it really is. Everyone's different. Everyone has something different to offer this world and everyone's got a talent, everyone's got weaknesses, and everyone has a story. It's important to give everyone a fair shake and a clean slate.

I love people because there are tons of good ones and you see how they're able to impact people's lives and I love being that type of guy too. If I can impact someone's life positively, that gives me so much joy.

When you get "that feeling"

To be honest, I don't have any regrets. I think I did everything that I was supposed to do, given the circumstances. I think I beat the odds academically and athletically. I did what I had to do. They say there are only a few times in your life when you get "that feeling," like when you get married or have your first child, but when I came out of my last final at the College of William and Mary, I got that feeling.

I had been paying my own bills since I was sixteen years old. I worked thirty hours a week all through high school and while playing football in college. Now coming from where I've come from to where I am today, I feel complete. I'm done, I'm finished. I earned a Bachelor of Arts and Sciences degree majoring in economics from the College of William and Mary and the Inspiration Award from my brothers on the football team. I am so happy.

Today Raeshawn is putting his economics degree to good use. He lives in Northern Virginia where he is a Recruiter for Signature Federal Systems and is pursuing his future as a financial representative with Primerica.

Aden Withers
Celebrate Every Success

I have wanted to publicly share my story for a long time. It's not a fairy tale; it's actually quite tragic. I could share the sordid details of my treatment and abuses, but that's not my agenda.

I want to share my thoughts on aging out of foster care. I want to help make the process better for others, and I want to inspire current foster children aging out to keep trying even when it feels like you can't.

Briefly, my story includes the removal of me and my brother from our mother's care at the age of fourteen and twelve, respectively.

She was drug addicted and could not care for us. Unfortunately for us, our social worker separated us geographically. He was placed with his dad about 12 hours away in a different province of Canada.

We had very little, to no contact, due to the fact, my social worker kept us geographically apart. I experienced seven foster care homes with good, bad, and terrible experiences with the government representatives who were supposed to be helping and protecting me. Some of these experiences I am still coping with today, and others I may carry with me forever.

Being an adult sometimes sucks. It's more challenging when you have complex post-traumatic stress disorder and other mental health issues. It is quite frankly tougher than the feeling of loneliness that you get when you see a *normal* child with their blood parents while you sit by your foster parents' or social worker's side.

I work a minimum wage job, and I pay bills. I don't have the education I want yet, but I cannot let that allow me to believe I am not successful. I can't blame that on the fact that the foster care system is flawed. I can only blame myself for so long—until I realize that success is not measured always in how much money you make, but also how you work on yourself.

Now, a little personal story.

I tried to report sexual abuse when I was younger and had a social worker not believe me. They even tried to say I was causing public mischief. It caused so much pain in me that I continue to feel bad about it today, despite my case being in court. I need constant reassurance that I am believed in order to live each day. Some social workers are corrupt.

That being said, if it weren't for the one social worker in the room with me who believed me, I would not have survived today. Her reassurance and comforting meant the world to me in the darkest times.

It's hard out there in the real world.

For a long time, I was angry. The foster care system did not prepare me for the adult world. I was angry because I don't have the cushion of parents to fall back and rely upon after coming of age.

I was angry at "the system" for not preparing me, but in hindsight my journey had just begun. They showed me how to pay bills and file taxes. I admit I was lucky there. But I had to be motivated to do it. I had to get up and go to those appointments and seminars and attend them knowing that I wasn't going to get any short-lived reward like a candy or maybe a gift card or some food.

My reward was preparing me to become the adult I am now.

I have worked minimum wage, entry level jobs, and I have learned how to pay bills and keep my head above water. The fact that I am still alive, off the streets, with a high school diploma was my reward for attending those meetings. It's so easy to be angry and slip into the world of drug addictions and jail.

It's so easy to be angry at the system when they have wronged you personally. Sometimes it's easier to do that than to face the reality of what being an adult really means.

It's easy to not care and to give up or be in jail. It's easy and some days I honestly wish I would've given up the moment I moved into my own first apartment. Some days I want to kick and scream and throw myself on the ground like a child.

Some days, I actually do have childlike tantrums. Some days I want to give up and take something to ease the burdens that I face. But then I remember that everything I face is only temporary, and that all of my problems can be solved if I just take baby steps into the adult world to achieve my goals.

In order to do that I must continue to pay my bills and work my job. I must continue to stay sober and focused. If I want to have a good life, the most important thing I must do is simply exist for another day.

It's hard coming out from foster care and not having that cushion of family to rely upon, but I think the hardest part for me was just realizing that I don't have it, and not the actual part of not having that cushion.

It's hard realizing that in the real world, a lot of people don't care that you were a hurting child and now are a hurting adult. All they care about is if you show up for work and do the job. I know that you have hopes and dreams and goals, but those successful people didn't just go from high school to a great job. They had to take baby steps in the right direction.

They, like the rest of us, had to wake up each morning and continue to exist in order to reach their goals.

Wake up every day with a dream

There is a difference between a foster care survivor and a foster care victim. Survivors don't always have to be these great, successful, and rich people. They can be the people who wake up every day with a dream in their head on where they want to go and who they want to be and still have minimum wage jobs where they flip burgers to make ends meet.

A foster care victim could be the most successful person in the world and still not have the strength and courage to continue to exist like we survivors do the next day.

A survivor has meltdowns and bad days and even relapses into old habits, but the difference between a victim and a survivor is that when a survivor gets knocked down, they get right back up and continue to exist, whereas a victim will give up and cease to exist.

I am a survivor with hopes and dreams. I dream of a better life for my son. I dream of a better system for foster children in Canada. I dream of healing my soul and finding peace in my life. I have shared my journey with legislators, lawyers, and more.

I want foster children to have a better safety net when they age out of care, access to mental health assistance, and proper safe housing. I am actively suing the Ministry of Children and Families to ensure no child gets treated the way I did. This advocacy and my son keep me moving forward.

It's important to understand that you are somebody's friend, family member, or community member and your existence matters to this world.

Inside your head are ideas and dreams that nobody else in this entire world has ever, or will ever, think of or dream of because they are inside you and you are important. You can ignite the world with those ideas and dreams, or you can let them flicker and die. Your ideas and dreams don't deserve that flicker as recognition, and neither do you.

Calling all foster care adults to be survivors here.

You are my people.

The people who know what it feels like to be unwanted.

The people who know laws better than most lawyers.

The people who have survived a system up until this point, that sadly many have not.

The people that know what it's like to dream of being something like an astronaut while flipping burgers at a fast-food place.

You are the people who know what it feels like to celebrate every success, whether big or small, even if that success means that you are still breathing right now.

Image courtesy of Now Media Group

Aden Withers is a twenty-six-year-old First Nations person who resides in British Columbia, Canada with their child. On January 27, 2020, Aden reached a settlement with the Kelowna Royal Canadian Mounted Police (RCMP), and the Ministry of Child and Family Development (MCFD) for neglecting care and sexual harassment. Through this settlement and going public, Aden has become a strong advocate for Indigenous children in care and sexual abuse survivors. One of Aden's greatest achievements was helping aid in the establishment of a sexual assault unit in the Kelowna RCMP. Aden is a dedicated advocate and continues to do work in their community.

Jon Ortiz
Starting My Own Story

Okay, well, I'm originally born first generation Dominican. I lived in New Jersey with my mother, her sister, and my cousin.

We would visit my dad twice a year in the Dominican Republic. He came over when I was in the second grade and we moved to Pennsylvania. That was when the tension started because my parents were from a different country, with three children, living in Pennsylvania and working in New Jersey.

It was a two hour commute each way for them. My little brothers went to daycare in New Jersey while my mom worked. I raised myself for a while because I got up, went to school, came home, and I was alone at the house until about 7:30, 8:00 p.m. every night.

It was pretty tough. Money was scarce.

My dad grew up in the Domincan Republic, so his way of parenting and discipline was different than is legal here. He was an abusive guy. When I look back now, he always wanted to be the Alpha, the Man. It was a cultural thing. If I got in trouble at school, that would in his eyes, justify abuse.

So, two weeks before graduating from fourth grade I was put in foster care.

My father was arrested for the initial abuse. It was severe. He broke my arms with a piece of railing. The court order said that he couldn't come anywhere near me.

The cops saw my dad's car near my house, and they asked me, "Hey, has your dad been at your house?"

At first, I said *no*. I probably continued to say *no* for 30 minutes because I have two younger brothers and I knew we could be separated, and I didn't want that.

My teacher was in the same room with me, and he said, "If you can't help us, we can't help you."

So, I admitted that my dad was at the house. They go to the house and arrest him. My mom hears about it at work and she calls me at the Boys and Girls Club, where I had been going since my dad was arrested the first time.

She says, "Did you tell? Did you? Did you tell the cops?"

I said *no, Mama, I didn't.*

She proceeded to say, "You just wait till I get home."

So, I'm in Boys and Girls Club and I know I have three hours of freedom until something bad goes down. I tell you, those three hours, man, they were... it was problematic for me.

I just want to run away. I think, for the first time, I prayed. I truly prayed for that time to go slow. I did not want my mom to get there. I did not.

My mom brings me home and she puts my brothers upstairs and she ties my hands together and she puts them in a pot of boiling hot water and she's walking me through what I am supposed to say the next day in court.

She says, "You're going to tell the Judge that he never broke your arms and you lied about him being in the house."

She said I was mad at my dad, and every time I said *no*, she would put my hands in the boiling hot water.

That was the second time that day I wanted to run away.

She kept walking around furious, yelling, telling me to keep my hands in the water. She had a belt or a broom with her and she would hit me with it when I took them out too early.

I could see my school bag in the laundry room, and I was thinking I could run right now. But I didn't.

The next day at school, my teacher looks at me, looks at my hands, and starts asking questions. I keep my mouth shut. He takes me to the nurse's office, and they ask what happened. Again, I'm not saying anything, and they are just, *all right, his dad's not in the picture because he is in jail.*

So, the only other person is his mom. Was she the one that did this? And I finally admitted it. I didn't know it, but that was the last day that I would walk out of my house. Straight after school, social workers took me to a foster home. My brothers were taken somewhere else.

Honestly, my first foster parents were a nice couple, but you can tell quickly that they had a way to discipline their foster kids. The father gave me his opening lecture and pretty much told me there was order in the home and I wouldn't disrupt it. He knew what went on in the house and so don't try him.

I had to go to school and act like everything was normal. Nobody around me understood what was going on.

I am that kid, my life had changed overnight, and nobody knew about it except the adults, but I'm not hanging out with the adults. It's not the adults I have recess with. It's not the adults I have lunch with. It's not like I have a quick thirty second story. I didn't have the energy to tell anyone about it.

I was thinking *why is everybody coming to school normal and smiling?*

I'm trying to figure out… what's going to happen after school? I think one of the biggest things about the transition period between an abusive home and a foster home, is you never know what is going to happen after school.

I have all these questions that are just unanswered. Why is this happening? What did I do to deserve this? They're questions that nobody can answer. People keep telling me *it's not your fault.*

But how can you say that when I'm the one who told the cops my dad was there and I'm the one that told that my mom was the one putting my hands in hot water?

I reported everything that led to the arrest, to more abuse, and to a broken home. I think that's a great tactic to tell kids that it's not their fault, but they need to say more than that.

I'm still worrying about my brothers when my caseworker asks me if I want to be with them. I did, so I was moved to a Dominican home and that was a good situation. It felt good to be with my brothers. There were some struggles.

The first twenty-four hours are the most important hours in a new foster home because in order for me to feel secure, I have to get around the house. I have to understand each person's way.

That's when you decide whether you are going to talk or not. It's one thing to answer a question. It's another thing to actually talk to them.

I'll be honest with you, it was good.

The family had very strict rules and at one point I learned, okay, this is the way it must be in a foster home. You have to set rules for strangers in the house.

My younger brothers are good, so that is easing my pain a little bit, until the day I came home from school and my caseworker is there and tells us to pack our bags because our aunt has just taken custody of us.

I'm not sure of the process but I trust the courts, so I take my brothers upstairs. We each pack our bags. So excited! This is my aunt that I don't really see that often, but I know its family, we're okay.

"Your aunt asked for them, not you."

Great! Come downstairs. We're each walking out and my caseworker asks me, "What are you doing?" I'm like, I'm just walking out and he's like, "Oh, your aunt asked for them, not you."

That, for me, was the worst thing that could ever happen to me.

Knowing my aunt made all the effort to go to the court, talk to a judge, talk to the police, and go through the whole process, just to ask for my brothers and not me. At that moment, watching my brothers leave, and this time knowing that it was because they were wanted, and I wasn't, was just heartbreaking.

This was my transition. I said to myself, all right, your brothers are safe with family. Family doesn't want you. Now, it's time for me to just do everything for myself, but why? Then I stopped. I've asked myself why so many times. So, at that time, I decided to stop asking questions and just started doing.

I was tired of having unanswered questions.

I was tired of people.

I was tired of moving.

I was tired of people not wanting me.

I was emotionally drained.

I was frustrated.

I was finished.

If this is the way it is meant to be, then everything from here on out is for me. Everything from here on out is to make me happy. That was like my breaking point, right there. That was like, okay, now I'm living day to day and I will make myself happy. I'm no longer of the mindset that my family is going to come save me.

I'm done

Normally, I'm the one with the mindset that I'm loved. At that point in time, mindset wise, I am not loved and I'm not going to whine about this because I'm done. I'm done asking questions. I'm done relying on somebody else to help me.

What made me happy? That summer I played baseball with a kid down the block. I practiced football with my foster family's oldest kid who was home from college, and I read.

I wasn't a very good reader at the time, but my social worker gave me a book called, *A Child Called It* by David Pelzer and I could relate to it. I realized that I wasn't the only one going through something like this. I could have gone the angry route or been self-destructive. I could have done stupid things as a kid and people would have said, *but he struggled.*

But my mindset at the time was, I can, not only can I get through this, but who am I, to just not do anything? Who am I, to not make something of myself? There's not much you can do as a 12-year-old, but when I read that book and realized that he had been a survivor and written a book, in my mind he was a success.

I could sit there and say, *oh pity me*, but what I learned in foster care, was once you hit adulthood no one is going to ask you what happened in your life. They won't say, *do you want to talk about it?* They are just going to say, *can you produce for us?*

When you apply for college, no one is going to ask you *what tormented your life?* They're going to ask, *are you going to keep up your grades or not? Are you going to pay us or not?*

Around that time, I felt like everybody was asking about my story.

I testified in court, talked to attorneys and social workers, my foster parents. I just kept repeating my story, and I just didn't want this to be my life.

I didn't.

I didn't want to continue to tell my story to everybody I met and get the same reaction of pity, pity, pity. At the time, with reading that book, I'm thinking, *nor will this be acceptable for long.* I can't just walk up to somebody and say, *oh, you should feel bad for me, now be my friend or do this for me.* That is just not going to work.

I'm tired of telling my story and at the same time knowing that there is a success story out there. I just wanted to start my own story, and I think that is what I've done ever since.

That was the same time that I was fortunate enough to get into the Milton Hershey School. Before everything happened, I think my mother had suggested it and then later my principal and social worker put in the application. I had an interview and got in!

I went to fifth grade for about a month in the public school and then on September 29, 2008, I started at Milton Hershey. Hershey created milk chocolate. He had failed in the chocolate industry for decades and was broke. Finally, he thought, let me put some milk in, and it went off. He and his wife, Catherine, were billionaires but they couldn't have kids, so they decided to create a school for orphan boys. They started with one farm home with fourteen or fifteen boys in 1909, and now it's a school for 2,500 kids – first boys, then they included girls, and now it's multicultural.

I'm taking a tour at the time and hearing how many times Milton Hershey failed.

He continued to persevere and then finally hit the jackpot. So here I am, a new student, right? I'm hearing all this and if his life isn't an inspiration to others, I don't know what is. There was literally inspiration all around me at the time.

I love that school! I graduated from there in 2016, so I was there for eight years. You have house parents in a home that has twelve boys or twelve girls. So here I am from foster care to a home of eleven other guys who are all in the same boat as me. Not all are from foster care. Some of their families visit on the weekend or pick them up. You have to meet certain criteria and be below a poverty line, but for me there was so much potential for success.

I had a roommate in the house. I had chores. I had expectations. They expect greatness from you. They know your situation, but they are not going to pity you.

I had a counselor when I went there. I met with her once or twice a week between fifth and eighth grade. Personally, my house dad, Mr. Messenger, helped me a lot. He knew what it took for kids to be successful. That was different for me, and it was life changing.

Getting my head straight

There's a lot of stigma with foster care. We were forced to grow up a little faster than others, but we knew it was going to be beneficial in some way for the rest of our lives. Foster care isn't going to be forever.

I was ready to work. I woke up at 5:30 every morning from the fifth to eighth grade to do a chore. The greatest thing that happened to me at that time was getting my head straight, away from negativity and more toward positive thinking.

My elementary school principal ended up adopting me when I was in the eighth grade. She had kept in contact with me. I would write her letters. When I would come home for holidays, I was spending half of the time with her and her family and the actual holidays with my foster family.

Statistically, I'm not supposed to be in college, but I steered away from the bad crowds, drugs, and illegal activities. I figured if it's not going to help me, then there is no point in doing it.

It will only make me stay in the situation of courts, judges, and lawyers that I am trying to get away from. I want to be a federal marshal. I met with a lot of police officers growing up. They were so engaging, talking to me, asking questions, taking me to court, picking me up at school. I knew from an early age that I loved police officers.

They would sit with me in the courtroom and just say, "It's going to be okay man. He's going to be in there. He's going to look at you. Don't worry about it. I'll be right behind him, so look at me. I will be with you at all times."

So, I gained a lot of respect for law enforcement.

I want to say to kids in my situation, don't ask too many *why* questions. More visualize what you want for yourself. So, start with asking yourself what you want to do, what makes you happy, and then start looking for it.

Jonathan Ortiz is a graduate student in the School of Public Policy at the Pennsylvania State University in University Park, Pennsylvania from which he also earned his Bachelor's of Science in Criminology. Through a lot of hard work and therapy, he has reconnected with his biological mother and has a loving relationship with his brothers. Jonathan hopes that adulthood allows him and his brothers to build on their relationship and be active in each other's lives. He thanks the Milton Hershey School for helping him flourish into a man but credits his adoptive mother for helping him realize his success in life.

Marie Boyd
No, I Don't Think So

My name is Marie Boyd. I was born in Puerto Rico, one of eight children. My father was in the military, which caused us to move to Virginia when I was eight. None of us spoke English.

We arrived here in the sixties when rebellion was a prevalent thing in the United States, but unacceptable in the eyes of my father, who had a deep-seeded belief that children should do exactly as he said.

He learned harsh corporal punishment from his people. My older siblings tried to protect the younger ones, but it didn't always happen.

One day I was walking home from school and I stopped at a garage where there was a Christian meeting of young people singing and praising God. I thought it was so interesting. I was meeting God in a whole other way than my Catholic upbringing.

I went home and joyfully told my parents what had happened. They rebuffed me, and the end result was a hit on the head with a metal object, and I was bleeding profusely. My parents wouldn't get me medical treatment. I was scared because things like this had happened hundreds of times, so I slipped out the window and went to a neighbor and told.

Social Services came to my house and I was taken to a juvenile detention center. I was treated like a criminal, handcuffed, and given a jumpsuit. When I appeared before a judge. he told me that, based on what he was seeing, and the number of years I had been in my home, I was going to be an alcoholic and abuser like my dad and I wasn't going to survive this.

I didn't believe what that judge said. I said to myself, *no, I don't think so.*

I was sent to a Christian drug rehab facility for two weeks until they found a foster family for me. I didn't want to leave. It was a wonderful place. But I had to go.

My social worker drove me down a very long road, until we reached a mansion and I thought, *oh wow, look at this!* I was scared and anxious. I saw a girl, who turned out to be my new foster sister and a man from the SPCA in the big front yard trying to get a cat out of a tree. They let us help, which disarmed some of my fears.

We went in and I met my foster parents who I learned were Mennonites with a very deep faith, plus they owned half of the city. They introduced me to their two teenage children who seemed to be very happy.

My foster mother said, "I'm glad you're here and if you need something just let us know. We will provide for you. You don't have to worry about eating or money. If you want to see your family, we will ask the social worker and she can arrange it when it is allowed."

Don't lie, cheat, or steal

She explained the rules, which were very simple; don't lie, cheat, or steal and you're going to be fine. Their home was different for me.

I had a bedroom with a TV stuck in a hole in the wall. It was all very fancy and a big change to get used to.

As time went on, I found that they genuinely wanted me there, but I didn't want to be there.

I wanted to be with my family, yet I knew what I would face if I went back. I was really torn.

It was time to go back to school. I had a new address, and most people didn't know I had changed families. My brothers and sisters who went to that school certainly knew, and they were upset with me. I was the only child removed from the home.

I suffered wondering if I had done the right thing.

All I remember is turning to my faith every time I struggled. From the time I was born, the Catholic community had taught me that God loved me and now this whole other religion is telling me that God loves me. He cares. So that was my one stop I always went to. I think that is one of the major reasons I made it through. I never lost faith that God had control of what was happening to me.

I was eleven, and I wanted so badly to have control over my life, and I missed my family so much that I even thought of running away. Then I remembered what my foster mother had said, *if you want to see them, I will take you.*

That was really the first test. I said to myself, *is she really going to do that?*

My foster mother consulted my social worker and she drove me to my family's home, but she did not come in. I discussed with my brothers and sisters that I didn't have a choice about living with them and if there was abuse at home now, they should leave too. I felt like I was empowering them.

My mother said that after I left, she had the nerve to tell my father that the way he treated us wasn't right so he couldn't live there anymore. I thought *okay, now I can go back home.* The abuser is gone. I talked to my social worker. She was really nice.

I realized social workers pick those jobs because that is what they want to do. I leaned on her for guidance and I listened intently to what she said because I felt she had my best interest at heart, even though she said things I didn't want to hear, like *no, you can't go home right now* and that I would have to *be patient.*

The goal of the foster care system is to return you to your family. That sounded good and logical to me.

I kept remembering what that judge had said about me, and I made a promise to myself that I was going to do two things.

First, I wanted to regain my freedom and have control over my life. The only way I could accomplish that was to follow the rules and ask for help to work toward my freedom. The other thing was to prove to that judge that he was wrong about me.

I learned a big lesson from my foster sister. She got pregnant and wasn't married. I knew that all hell was going to break loose because that is what would have happened in my old home. One night, we are all eating together and discussing family issues. I was terrified that my foster sister was going to be kicked out of the house.

That's when my foster mother announces, "we're having a baby and we are so excited." She wanted my sister to know that she was loved. I thought that was pretty cool. They were happy when the baby was born and came home to be part of our family. I started to realize that in life not everything that starts out bad ends up bad. Everything does not have to end tragically.

I was getting older and adjusting more and more to my life. My foster mother taught me the ins and outs of boys and relationships. What I didn't know then, but I do now, is that I was always looking for a father in my life. Although I had a foster father, he didn't say a lot, we didn't do much together. I respected him and he treated me fine, but he wasn't a Brady Bunch kind of dad.

Subconsciously, I was looking for that in boyfriends, which was not a good thing. I probably got taken advantage of by some people. When I would get really down, I would always say, *okay, it's just one day. Let's see what tomorrow brings. I will make a new adventure tomorrow.* I'm a big adventure girl!

I had become a person who didn't believe in herself

My foster mother drove me to school every day. Sometimes I would go behind the building and cry because my sadness was still deep down inside, and I missed my family. I just wanted to be normal.

One day, a gentleman, Mr. Tyson, walked up and asked me why I was crying. I told him I missed my family, and I wanted a job, and I just wanted to be normal. I was just about 16 and he told me, well if you want a job like the other kids, I will give you a job. Get your driver's license and you can be a student aid in the Driver's Education Program.

I was so happy I had opened up and answered him honestly. I could have kept my sorrow to myself and I never would have found Mr. Tyson. I got my first job and worked for him for three or four summers. He gave me a confidence that I had never had before. Before Mr. Tyson came along, I had become a person who didn't believe in herself.

Each person I let in along my journey helped me gain confidence. Mr. Tyson is one of the reasons that I am who I am today. He believed in me. When you're going through foster care, you can get a sense of being lost and when you feel lost, you have to turn not to yourself but to others to find your way. I turned to God first, and he was helping me. Then I also reached out to others. I learned to keep asking. There is no harm in asking for help and reaching for help.

Before I graduated, my foster parents decided to move to Canada. They wanted me to go too, but since I didn't want to leave, a new home was found for me while I finished high school. They also told me that the money they had been given through Social Services had been saved to give me when I graduated.

I was taken aback. I finally believed that they took me because they really wanted me.

When you're in foster care, you have a lot more on your plate than other kids. I wasn't studying as much or giving my best all the time to my classes. The result was I missed graduating on time by one tenth of a point.

I reached out to Mr. Tyson who said, "one tenth of a point? Go to summer school!"

While I didn't get to graduate with my class, I did graduate. Not graduating on time was a consequence of my actions. Had I done what I was supposed to do in those classrooms, it wouldn't have happened. In hindsight, my teachers went out of their way to help me, but they couldn't just give it to me. So, I went back and earned my high school diploma in summer school and made the decision to become a police officer.

Sometimes the devil would come in and tell me I wasn't wanted.

I had to fight against that. There was also peer pressure to do things that I knew I shouldn't do. Then I would remember what that judge said, and I was so determined to prove to that judge, and to myself, that I am the person that I decide I'm going to be.

However, before I finished high school, I transitioned to a new home and a very, very bad thing happened to me there.

Unfortunately, my foster father decided he wanted to have his way with me. I was looking for a father figure and believed that adults always know the right thing. Now I know they don't. My social worker questioned me because I stopped smiling as much. I thank God for a worker who was doing his job. I told him what happened.

He had me pack my things immediately. Since I was about to turn 18, I became an emancipated minor. Social Services helped me get an apartment and I had the money my first foster parents had saved for me.

Happily, after I graduated from high school and while living in my very own, first apartment, I entered and completed the Police Academy. To my surprise, my family found out about it and showed up for my graduation. It was a wonderful reunion.

Over time, I reconnected with each of my parents and have forgiven my father the way I know God forgives me. I can't imagine not forgiving somebody. Both of my parents have died, but today my husband and I care for my aging foster mother here in Virginia.

I've been married twice. First, for a short time, and I had a child. Later, while attending school to become a paralegal, I met my current husband whose family is loving and nurturing and accepted my daughter immediately as theirs. We had two more girls together.

Turn to somebody you can trust

Between reaching out and my faith, I turned a lot of dark moments into rainbows. I used those strategies starting as an eleven-year-old trying to figure out how to navigate a turned around life.

My social worker helped me a lot. I would ask her for help in handling situations unique to foster kids, like other kids teasing you. I tell kids all the time, reach out to your social worker, they care about you.

I also looked to my guidance counselors. They were wonderful. Turn to somebody you can trust. Make a connection with people. The more help and advice you get the better. I am very upset when people say they made poor choices or committed crimes because they were abused. I know that can be legitimate if they never got help.

When you don't get help, you get angry.

I have asked and received so much help over the years.

Just be you. Believe in yourself.

Protect your heart by not believing the negativity. You didn't do anything wrong.

You are a saved child. You have been saved from a bad situation and now you're under the umbrella of special foster child. You can tell others you are a foster kid because someone chose you and loves you extra special, and then show how special you are.

I am who I am because I was a special foster kid.

Trained as a police officer and paralegal, Marie Boyd, had brief careers in both fields before becoming a full-time volunteer chaplain to the Newport News, Virginia Fire Department. Following twenty years of service, where she was fondly known as Chaplett, she became a chaplain to the Sheriff's Department of Newport News. She began a non-profit, the Hampton Roads Good Samaritan Fund, in 2001, whose mission is to provide donations from people like YOU to help our neighbors through crises such as unpaid bills and illness, and at other times of need.

Marie has been married to Wesley Boyd for thirty-four years. They have three adult daughters, Kristina, Elizabeth, and Meredith. In 2014, she was named the Daily Press Citizen of the Year for her tireless work serving as a bridge between those who need help and those who want to help. Marie says her goal is to live simply but comfortably, and she wants others in the community to be able to do the same.

Chauncey Strong
Triplets!

I was in foster care at a very young age. I was not even two yet when I was taken from my home.

My mom, my adoptive mother I should clarify, told me the story of my adoption when I was about sixteen or seventeen years old. She told me I was in the hospital with a severely burned hand by the caregivers in my first foster family home. I had been removed from my biological family, placed in the foster home, and then put into a third home after being treated for burns in the hospital.

That third home would become my permanent home. This is where the story takes an unexpected turn for my adoptive parents. It was at this point the social worker informed them that I had siblings; I was one in a set of triplets! My adoptive parents had no clue going into this situation that I even had siblings.

At first, they said no, they were not interested because they were already fostering another sibling set of four. My parents said *no, it was too many children.*

The social workers tried to convince my mom and dad that we would have been, had they adopted us, the first set of triplets adopted under what we now call the Adoption Subsidy Act. It would have allowed them to get financial support until we were eighteen or twenty-one years old; including medical expenses.

So, it was the first time in New Jersey that you could get money on a consistent basis for a long period of time for adoption with special needs. Adopting triplets fell under special needs, not that we were particularly ill or in need of special services.

However, my parents were still saying, *nope, nope, we're not going to do it.*

But, on the day that the social worker came to pick me up and take me back, something changed. My dad had gone off to work and left my mom home alone with me. I was crying and not wanting to go. She told me I ran upstairs and hid up under the bed and they were trying to pull me out from under the bed, but I was rolling around on the floor. Finally, she just said, "I'm going to do it."

She said her heart broke in that moment and while she wasn't clearly thinking that she was going to adopt all three of us, she didn't want to lose me. She said she knew it was right for us to be together as siblings, so she made an executive decision to adopt us. Now mind you, my daddy was still at work and no idea what he was coming home to that night.

I can't even imagine having grown up knowing that I had two brothers—triplets mind you—and we didn't know each other, and we didn't have contact with each other.

Instead, I have these wonderful memories now. It was not all joy. We fought, and we did all kinds of things like most siblings. The interesting part about my story, even though my brothers and I were triplets, they looked more like twins and I looked like their little brother.

It was such a distinction the way they looked. They were so close to each other too. They thought alike, and they would do things that were alike.

I remember thinking it might be possible that the social workers told my mom and dad we were triplets just to get us adopted together. I really wondered about that because it was such a distinction. They were slightly taller, and they just looked more like twins. I believe that they were placed in foster care together before we came to be adopted, but I don't have the records of their first foster care placements.

There was definitely a special connection between the two of them, but growing up, I was my mother's favorite child. Even though I was technically the youngest. I think that favoritism dynamic played out because I came into the home first and my mom wanted me first.

We were latch-key kids. My mom and dad had separated when we were in the fifth grade. I was going home and making sure we got inside and warmed up or cooked whatever little food we had. I made sure we had dinner and went to bed before she got home from her shift.

For the bulk of my childhood it was just the three of us growing up. It was huge for us to experience childhood with each other.

I mean, we had each other's backs. We didn't let anybody bother us outside of the three of us. It was this real sense of connection.

My mom raised us as a single woman in the heart of Newark, New Jersey. Drugs were a real problem, and I think she was determined not to let us fall into the wrong group or, worse, get killed. She found a way to put us in private schools from grade school through high school.

That was a big deal back in those days, but they gave her all kinds of financial assistance. Again, it was a big deal for the schools, too, because we were adopted triplets. It was written up several times, and they enjoyed the publicity. In fact, I found out later my grades weren't good enough to get into my high school, but my mom insisted they take all three of us.

I used to think, man, if I could just have half of their brains.

I worked very hard and earned C's while they didn't seem to study much and earned A's and B's.

I was happy to get out, but I worked hard. I eventually went to college and even graduate school too: that's where I really shined.

I never wanted to find my biological family

As close as the three of us were, we did differ greatly on our opinions of our biological family. Growing up, I never wanted to find my biological family.

In my mind, they didn't love us and if they did love us, then we would be in their home. And so, they must not have loved us.

My brothers on the other hand very much wanted to find our family. They believed that our family was out there looking for us. Our family was out there, and they could be rich, they could have money.

When my mom and dad divorced, we moved into low-income housing and although my mom was still getting a check, it was very little compared to what families are getting now, and even that is still very little. As I've said, living in the projects around Newark was a tough thing. My brothers almost had this fantasy that our biological family was going to be better and be able to provide for us once we found them, and so they went looking for my family.

We didn't really talk about adoption in my family. I think my mom came from the school of thought that "children were to be seen and not heard." We didn't have conversations with my family or my mom. She said to do something, and you did it however she wanted it done. Like this was pretty much it, so we never had adoption conversations.

As a child, I never knew anything about my biological family, I just assumed they didn't love us. Believing this allowed me to get through the next day and every day. I didn't want to dwell on the fact that we had these people out here.

My brothers looked much sooner for our biological family than I did. When I decided to look for my family it was like what you read in a book. I didn't want to find my family until I went to the doctor and the doctor started talking about my family medical history. I started talking about my adoptive family history.

I realized that I had better clarify that I was speaking about my adoptive family because I didn't know my biological family. The doctor took the paper he was writing on and threw it away, he discarded all that information and he said, *you know, that's not your family medical history.* He said, *I know you love your family.* I knew what he was saying. He didn't even have to say it, but I knew exactly where he was going because your family medical history is with your biological family.

I said I really don't know them, and he advised me to start by just doing some blood work and then start creating a medical file.

I knew about my brothers and so at least I had that kind of information. That's when I thought, even if it's for just medical reasons, maybe I should try to find my family.

Ironically, when I went back to find my family it was actually well documented, because we were one of only a few other triplets born in New Brunswick, New Jersey and the first set adopted under the new adoption plan.

I spoke with a state worker about our records and they were able to find some pictures also. She told me she tried to send the information to my brothers a few years earlier.

She said every time they sent my brothers something, they were moving around so much it would be returned. She sent everything that I was looking for. It just shows that even though I think my brothers and I were close; we had a different feel about what was happening for us in the realm of being adopted.

I think my brothers held some resentment at my mother's affinity for me. I believe it drove them to find our real parents so that they could be more connected to our real parents. The sad part is, none of us were right about our story.

I thought that my family didn't love us.

My brothers thought our family loved us and they had money.

Neither of those were true.

I want to clarify that our birth family did love us, but they just could not take care of us.

My mom was twenty-two and she had already had a four-year-old child. The four of us were living with my grandmother and uncle, so there were seven, sometimes eight, people living in a two-bedroom apartment. There was never any abuse, but there was neglect.

She just couldn't take care of us, so we went into foster care. She was told she would still be allowed to see us and visit, but the record says that after several missed appointments, they terminated parental rights.

When my brothers learned this information, they realized we grew up pretty much in the same general area of where we were born. My mom went on to have two other children but remained fairly poor.

We all were doing so much better than they were.

So, it was a reality check for all of us.

In 2005, my brother Chadwick passed away. Sadly, we were fairly estranged from each other because we had gone to college in different states and, back then, we did not have cell phones and social media sites. We had to communicate using pen and paper. You wrote a letter, you hoped it got there, and if it didn't, you were out of luck. So, after college, we literally just lost contact with each other for a long time. I ended up having to do a search to find my own brothers.

The Salvation Army will help you find people

A lot of people don't know this, but the Salvation Army will help you find people.

The more information you know, the better. Of course, I knew their names, I knew their birth dates, and I knew their social security numbers.

Within a week they contacted me with their address in Idaho. I finally reconnected with them after ten years. I visited them a couple times before Chadwick entered the hospital. Within a few months, he passed away. Sadly, in 2008, my other brother, Clinton, also passed away.

Chadwick and Clinton had been so close, and I just felt Clinton needed me after Chadwick died. I asked him to come live with me. I wasn't married at that time, so I just thought it would be better for him than to be alone in Idaho.

They had had a card business, and he said he wanted to stay in Idaho to try to make a go of the business.

I share this story with foster youth and with foster and adoptive parents to illustrate the importance of sibling connections. My brothers are gone, but they're never truly gone from me. I always have these memories of them.

I thank God we were raised together for me to build at least thirty some odd years of memory of them so that they can live with me forever. It is tragic some young people in foster care don't know where their brothers and sisters are, or they are separated and can't communicate.

I understand that sometimes it is a difficult situation, but I don't always agree with why siblings are separated.

I say to foster parents, CASA, judges, I'm just one story that's like this.

There are thousands of kids who are in foster care who are not placed with their siblings and some don't even know where their siblings are living.

Let's let them have at least childhood memories that can lead to longer-term connections. The sibling connection piece is a big one for me. My hope for young people in foster care is that they never stop advocating for their siblings. Ultimately the best thing for them is to have some type of connection with them or visitation with them, seeing them on a frequent basis, and utilizing all forms of communication including social media and Skype.

Bridging The Gap

I do a training called "Bridging The Gap," that talks about the importance of foster families and birth families working together.

I held my own Bridging The Gap in 2009 when I married my second wife. I brought my two families together at our wedding and I jokingly told people, "I want y'all to come, but I don't want any drama because I paid a lot of money for this wedding."

Not only was there no drama, but they hung out with each other and talked and shared stories. The one thing they had in common was me, and they were willing to come together for that. I've been married for eight years, and we have a beautiful five-year-old daughter.

My brothers and my mothers are gone now, and I don't have the close family ties that some people have, but I do have some strong memories of them to carry with me and to share with my daughter.

Chauncey Strong, originally from Newark, New Jersey, earned his BA degree in Social Work from Elizabeth City State University, in Elizabeth City, North Carolina, in 1991 and his MSW from Norfolk State University, in Norfolk, Virginia, in 1993.

Chauncey is a child welfare advocate with twenty-five years of extensive experience in child welfare administration in the private and public sector and specializes in foster care and adoption training and consulting. Most recently he worked for eight years as a foster care supervisor with Fairfax County Department of Family Services in Fairfax, Virginia. He has also served as an administrator, manager, supervisor, child welfare worker, mentor, and a community organizer.

Chauncey is the Executive Director of Strong Training and Consulting, LLC where he provides training and consulting in child welfare. He is currently consulting with The Annie E. Casey Foundation, The Capacity Building Center for States, and The Virginia Department of Social Services.

Chauncey has served on several national boards and committees and is also a motivational speaker and a committed advocate for children and families. He has dedicated his career to helping to improve the outcomes of children and families involved in the child welfare system.

Maggie Rose Grimm
I Can Do More Than Survive, I Can Thrive

There are times in our life when it seems we have no hope; that darkness swallows us up only to spit us back out into the cold.

However, where there is darkness there is always light; and where there is light, there is hope.

Living with my divorced biological parents was absolute torture. I was abused physically, emotionally, and mentally by my mother every single day, and was sexually abused by a family member for a number of years, which my family knew about.

The fourteen years I spent bouncing from home to home where we didn't know if there would be electricity or food was excruciating, and that's why I decided to fight to be removed when I was fourteen.

Seeking shelter for two

I had a twin sister that I worried for, and I didn't want us to live a life of suffering and for a cycle to be repeated. That was when one day, I was being dropped off after school by my ninth grade Earth Science teacher, Jennifer (Jeffi) Connor. We were discussing my abuse, and she said she wanted to help me find some counseling. It was then that we decided I would go for an intake at my local women's and children's shelter and begin working on my mental health.

I remember sitting outside my house known in town as the "mold hole" and talking with Jeffi about my experience with the intake and how we were going to make therapy work.

She was the first person to ever help me realize that I deserved more from life; that I was worthy of being healthy and being cared for. She was the first person to jump-start my journey of getting out of my situation, and I owe her my life for it.

That's when my school librarian, Mike, and I had a conversation about us going to live with him and his wife, Mary. Jeffi, Mike, and I met in his office and talked about the abuse I was dealing with, and then discussed living with them. I was able to give statements to his attorney describing the abuse I was suffering and how my parents either participated or did nothing to stop it from happening. I went to court multiple times and spoke about how the abuse was occurring and how it affected me.

I would tell my mother that I was at a friend's house and then have that friend drop me off at the courthouse so I could be present for the hearing that would occur that day.

The hardest part was having to speak my truth in front of my mother, who had treated me with such cruelty, but I did it. After months of telling people just the surface of what had happened in my life, there came a time when I had to tell everything.

Two days into my sophomore year of high school, my twin sister and I had to go do an interview with a case worker about our situation, and I decided that we needed out. I poured out everything I had ever experienced to their listening ears for eight hours straight. It was the hardest thing I've ever had to do, but it was so liberating and worth it.

Removed

As a result, my sister and I were immediately removed and put into an emergency placement with a friend of ours for two days and then placed with Mike and Mary.

It was at this moment that I realized that I had POWER; that I had the ability to change my circumstances. While it was hard, it helped shape me into the person that I am today and eliminated the hurt and pain that I had gone through for so long. It helped me learn that I have people who truly care for me and want the best for me, and they do so because they know what I need and put that above their wants. People like Mike and Mary.

Mike and Mary went through the long process of earning their foster care license just so my sister and I could stay with them. I was fortunate enough that they were the only placement I ever experienced.

It was difficult to get used to at first. I was diagnosed with PTSD, chronic anxiety, and depression when I was fourteen. These things made it difficult to change the thoughts I would tell myself about myself.

Getting used to having rules and expectations was difficult. There were many times when I had my car, that I would go places without telling Mike and Mary where I was, and they would get worried. I didn't understand why they were so worried about me, as my biological parents never really cared where I went and what I was doing. There were many times while living with my dad that I would leave for hours and go to the library, and he never once asked me where I was going or how long I would be gone.

While it was hard to adjust to a "normal" life, I accepted it with open arms, and on March 7, 2019, I was officially a legal member of their family through adult adoption. They are the best thing that could have happened to me, and they love me unconditionally.

Create a life you deserve

The purpose of telling you this backstory is so that you can understand that going into care wasn't the easy thing that seems to be portrayed through the media. I, like many other foster kids, had fought SO hard to be removed, and it worked.

You should never give up on creating a better life for yourself. You DESERVE to be loved, cared for, and cherished. You are not your past; you are not your parents; you are not your circumstances.

You are worth so much more.

One of the programs that really helped me realize that I can do more than just survive, but that I could thrive, was the Seita Scholars Program at Western Michigan University. I was talking with my Michigan Youth Opportunity Initiative coordinator when she mentioned that there was a program at WMU that supported former and current foster kids. She told me that they provided substantial financial aid for students, as well as a support system full of coaches.

I applied as soon as I could, which ended up being during the beginning of my senior year of high school and was their first applicant for the 2016-2017 school year. I had gone for a tour of the campus with my foster parents, and as soon as I walked into the office, I knew that's where I needed to be.

The atmosphere was so welcoming, and everyone I saw said hello to me. This was when I met Ronicka for the first time. She immediately welcomed me to the office with a big smile and warm demeanor. I would later find out that Ronicka would be my campus coach, and she is the one who taught me that life didn't just have to be about the bad times and how they affected me negatively, but also about the positive attributes that I have as an individual.

We talked about what my good qualities were, but also about where I had "opportunities for growth." You see, the Seita Scholars Program focuses on what the student believes is best for them, while remaining a backbone of support when we need guidance.

Seita and Ronicka, as well as those who have shown support to me, taught me how to get the most out of life and not just go through the motions.

We are here on this planet to make connections with people and find our "people" – which is so important for any current or former foster youth.

For me, pursuing a degree in Family Studies at Western Michigan University has really helped me find those who genuinely care about me and my future.

Seek and find

The common theme I want you to take away from this, is that you must seek out and find those who see your worth for what it is: invaluable. You are worth being cared for, worth being loved, and you most certainly deserve to thrive in life.

Remember that you, dear reader, are the guiding force for your own destiny. Work through your fears and hesitations and find those that will help you do so. There are good people out there in the world; not everyone is going to hurt you, and most would want to help you.

You can do this. I did it, my best friend did it, as well as so many others! Don't let your history and your circumstance determine what you deserve in this life. As my amazing therapist says, "All you have to do is live well, and you've won." It won't be easy, but the worthwhile stuff rarely is.

Ronicka, left, and Maggie, right, on campus

Maggie Grimm is originally from Fowlerville, Michigan. Following is her biography in her own words.

I am a Junior going into my last year at Western Michigan University in Kalamazoo, Michigan. I am majoring in Family Studies and minoring in Communication. After I finish my bachelor's I will go on to obtain my Master's in Counseling Psychology! I love to work closely with the Seita Scholars Program to bring awareness to foster care and how we can aid students in pursuing a higher education! I am so grateful for the Seita Scholars Program and how much they have helped with finances, housing, mental and physical health, and so much more! I will be forever indebted to my parents, Mike and Mary Grimm, for taking me in when I needed it the most. I'm grateful for Ronicka, the director of our program, for giving her all and leading our team these past few years and believing in me so fiercely. To my best friend Halana for being by my side through college and through all my ups and downs, thank you. I am also so grateful to my therapist Tami for believing in me and teaching me how to live well. Her impact is why I am able to participate in this book. I love all of you and am so grateful! Lastly, I am thankful for those who participated in this book and for those who are still searching for their voice. You can do this. Find your tribe!

Terry Morris
All I Have Is Today

I am inquisitive by nature. I have spent a lifetime asking why and seeking answers from teachers, ministers, professors, and family members.

My questioning nature is why I am who I am today: NASA scientist, father, husband, and an advocate for children in crisis. It is also the source of my resilience to endure my abandonment in Tupelo, Mississippi at the age of thirteen in 1980.

I grew up 587 miles north of Tupelo, Mississippi in Chicago, Illinois. My single mother was raising three boys and two girls. I was the second oldest and most closely resembled my absent father. This coupled with my questioning nature was reason enough for my mother to take out her frustrations in life on me.

It did not take long for my siblings to catch on that I was an easy target for scapegoating anything that could get our mother upset. Whatever went wrong must be Terry's fault. Often, the consequences did not match the "crime." I earned a B+ instead of an A, I asked a question in church, or I asked why one too many times. My childhood was full of beatings, homelessness, and hunger.

Later in life, I learned from a psychologist that my mother was experiencing psychological transference. She most likely was not consciously reacting to me as if I were my father, but my resemblance to him was a trigger to her that I was not good.

She would look at me and see the child who looks like her ex-husband she dislikes and end up beating, hitting, cursing out this child for something someone else did and not even be aware that she was doing it. I think there's a lot that happened to me through psychological transference. It was confusing and painful. I learned that I had to suppress my questioning nature when I was in the presence of my mother.

The crocodile who gives the fox a ride

My story has similarity to the parable about the crocodile who gives the fox a ride across the river then promptly eats him at the shoreline after promising not to eat him. The crocodile's nature is to eat smaller animals, not rescue them.

My nature was to ask questions, not stifle them. And so eventually I was kicked out of the house for the last time in 1980 at the age of thirteen. I was dropped off on a dirt country road in Plantersville, Mississippi (a small town outside Tupelo, Mississippi). I sought shelter in barns and fields and foraged for food in trash cans and backyard gardens. I walked up and down the country roads, and there was just nothing but time, literally nothing but time to just think, to think about my life.

Every now and then I would come across a little country church, and at least back in the deep South of Mississippi, they would have these churches dotted along the country roads. I remember the distance between the houses was miles, and these scattered churches all had little grave sites.

I'd sit there looking at the headstones of these long dead people and wonder about their lives.

I'd be looking at them and thinking, *wow, one day I'm going to be there.* I would look at the little dash between the date of birth and date of death and wonder what happened in between. I would wonder if any of these people who died had problems with their parents when they were in this world, would that have mattered?

They're dead now.

What complaints did they have about life? Perhaps they had some control over their life, maybe they didn't have complete control over their life, but they had at least a little bit of influence in their own lives. What did they do with the influence that they had?

As I looked at the grave sites, a light bulb turned on inside me. I realized these people had a lot of choices. They probably had more choices than they realized. So now I look at my life eating out of garbage cans and sleeping wherever I can find a soft place for my head. I have no change of clothes.

I question myself. *Do I have choices?*

And I realized that I did, and the choice that I had was to decide to make something of my life. I did not know how I would achieve it, but I had to make something of my life. Like most teenagers, I had no idea what I wanted to do, and I knew even less about how to go about doing it. How does one go about getting an education in my circumstance?

I thought that I had little control of that part, but the part I could control or at least influence was my internal dialogue.

I realized that there are internal choices that we have. I know we are aware of it, but we may not be as cognizant and bring it to the forefront, so we can be clear about the choices that we have. I would hear my biological mother's voice telling me I was stupid. I was ignorant. I would never amount to anything.

Everything is your fault. These things that bothered me the most were internal more than anything else. These harsh words played in my head over and over. I started questioning the negative thoughts that came to me.

I began to visualize this invisible part of my brain as a garden.

Weeds growing in my garden

The negative comments from my mother were like weeds growing in my garden.

She had planted seeds of destructive weeds in my garden.

When you're a child, you don't know what your parents are planting. Some parents plant seeds by reading bedside stories to you or by encouraging you to be strong or independent. Other parents plant seeds of doubt or hate. But when you get to a certain age of where you can decide for yourself, and this is the hard part, you must make decisions to establish your garden to fit your desires and goals.

Well, why am I talking about this crazy stuff? Who's responsible for your heart? When you start thinking like that, you realize that you do have an incredible amount of influence. If somebody plants a bad seed, you remove that seed from your garden. Sometimes you have got to work hard to undo the seeds.

But if that's the type of garden you want, you must work to remove the bad seeds and keep the good ones.

There is a psychological and emotional amount of work that nobody can seem to get out of. When I analyzed the healthy families, the children are so blessed because the parents have already structured the environment for them. They are protecting the garden of both the mind and the heart of their children.

It is not to say that there's not a genetic component, but there's an agenda coupled with a genetic component, and at least they're doing everything they can to protect the kids.

As I started realizing this, I began to understand that I have a littered garden; people have screwed up my freaking garden!

This was my epiphany.

I didn't fully comprehend the depth of this revelation, but I did know that I could work on fixing my garden. I got the essence of it, that I do have some influence to change my life. I actually felt like I had been born anew. I knew that there's a physical garden, a ground, and there is a mental one, an emotional one.

I started realizing that the manifestations of a person's life over time are due to what other people have done to them and how they chose to respond to those actions.

This is not what I want

People will throw trash into my garden, but I can either leave those cans and broken bottles there or decide this is not what I want and remove it.

The fact that I must undo somebody else's trash is not fair, but this is my garden and you take ownership and responsibility of your garden. That's the garden of your heart and your mind, and that's why I cannot say how difficult that is for most people.

Especially if you're a teenager tossed back and forth through foster care and back and forth between families. It is hard. It sounds like magical thinking, but my garden analogy is not magical thinking, there is a true cause and effect relationship.

So, there I was sitting in a little cemetery in Plantersville reflecting on eating out of the garbage cans.

I'm upset.

I'm frustrated.

My family kicked me out and abandoned me and went back to Chicago like, *what are they doing right now?* While I'm angry, hungry, and vengeful, what are they doing? I think they're probably eating fried chicken and ice cream, macaroni and cheese, and I'm like, how? It was like an out of body experience.

I was looking at myself and asking *why am I holding onto all this negative emotion? They're just as happy without me.* They probably don't even care what they did was wrong, but I'm the one that's been victimized and abused, and I have all this anger.

I don't know where this thought came from, but it went something like this: I asked, *who am I hurting with all my anger and thoughts of revenge? Well, I'm not hurting anybody, I thought. I didn't ask to be here, and I got kicked out for no fault of my own. What choices did I have in all of this?* Then I realize who I am hurting; myself.

I may not have been able to control what other people have done to me, but I can influence my response. All I have is today. I don't have a time machine to go back and change anything. What can I do to make my life better today and ease the anger and the bitterness? Who am I hurting by holding onto this toxic, toxic waste? I am hurting myself.

When you start seeing life through those glasses, you make very different decisions than you would before. You realize you have control of how you respond and react.

I decided to choose not to put forth my energy in things that are not in my best interest. I realized that the only way that I could go forward was by making the best use of my mental, cognitive, and psychological resources.

I was not quite ready at that time, but later I grew to understand I needed to forgive also. Forgiveness is one of the healthiest things for us. Now I'm not blind. I'm not saying it's a panacea for everything, but there are many things that are stopping us from achieving a successful healthy life, but we can choose to forgive and let go.

I had to move on with my life. I didn't know what I wanted. I was like a person walking across the United States without a map and being asked, where are you going? I did not know. I just want to get somewhere positive. I don't want to have regrets. I don't want to look back on my life and say I would've, could've, or should've. I don't know when the opportunity comes, but whenever it does, I'm going to take advantage.

So, when the community of Plantersville had finally seen enough of me wandering their town and eating out of their trash cans, someone called the police, and social services placed me in Alpha House, a group home in Tupelo, Mississippi. I was put back in school, and I saw education as an opportunity.

Tomorrow's not promised to anybody

I tried to take advantage of every opportunity. I ran cross country and entered spelling contests. The other kids would ask why I was working so hard. I did not want to get to the end of school and just say I should have done this, I wanted to do that. Tomorrow's not promised to anybody. You must give it the best that you have, so that's been my life ever since.

So, in hindsight, I would say when my biological mother abandoned me in Mississippi, the thing that I thought was the worst, ended up being the best thing that could've ever happened to me. It got me out of this extremely negative, pessimistic environment, and it put me in a different environment with people who thought differently, who processed differently, who didn't just complain.

I want to forgive, and I want to live.

I want a good life, and I want to help others along the way.

I've learned the way that I want the world to be is the way I need to tend my garden. When I make my garden a certain way, I attract other people who similarly tend their gardens. I've learned to trust it. It took years with good and bad friends and staying with good and mediocre foster families.

I choose to see the best even though I know some of them didn't intend the best. While some families may not have treated me the best, at least they gave me a bed to sleep in. So even this foster family, who I didn't think I resonated well with and who I felt treated me unfairly, still treated me better than my biological family. I started focusing on the good in the situation instead of on the negative.

I didn't have to sleep outside. That's what allowed me to earn an education, participate in extracurricular activities, and run cross country. Sometimes I would call it the one eye closed disease: sometimes there are good things that are happening, but if you focus on just the negative, you overshadow the good thing. When you focus on the negative, you diminish the positive part and it's hard to sort of get both.

I've had both, and I think the quality of our lives is influenced by the one we choose to focus on the most.

Who do you choose to allow to influence you the most?

That's your decision.

When you realize that you have more influence over your internal garden, then you realize you still have a choice. I have a choice, and just even that choice gives hope.

Terry Morris was born in Chicago, Illinois to an extremely abusive family. He suffered child abuse from four years old until his abandonment in Plantersville (near Tupelo), Mississippi. He excelled at Tupelo High School and eventually started working at NASA a few days after his high school graduation. Terry is currently a systems engineer as well as a national speaker supporting philanthropy, education, community service, and child advocacy in multiple countries. Some of his national speaking engagements have included the White House, the Pentagon, the Federal Reserve, FBI, CIA, National Security Agency, NASA, OPM, the Smithsonian, the Nuclear Regulatory Agency, Selective Service, the National Institutes of Health, as well as the Departments of Justice, Agriculture, Interior, State, Treasury, and Transportation. He is the Lead for Integrated Hazard Analysis with-

in the Safety-Critical Avionics Systems Branch at the NASA Langley Research Center. He has received the White House's National CFC Hero Award as well as NASA's Exceptional Achievement Medal. Dr. Morris holds a Bachelor's degree in Electrical Engineering from Mississippi State University in Mississippi State, Mississippi, a Master's in Electrical Engineering from Old Dominion University in Norfolk, Virginia, a George M. Low Fellowship from the Massachusetts Institute of Technology in Cambridge, Massachusetts, a Ph.D. in System Engineering from the University of Virginia in Charlottesville, Virginia, a Certificate of Public Leadership from the Brookings Institution, in Washington D.C., and a Certificate in Architecture and Systems Engineering from the Massachusetts Institute of Technology. He is a Lifetime Associate Fellow of the American Institute of Aeronautics and Astronautics (AIAA) as well as the Director of the Information Systems Group. Dr. Morris also serves as the President of the Virginia Peninsula Food Bank.

Sophia Booker
Full Circle: From Foster Child to Foster Leader

My name is Sophia Booker, and I am studying for my Master's in Social Work at Virginia Commonwealth University.

I also work for Project LIFE (Living Independently Focusing on Empowerment), a program with United Methodist Family Services that focuses on permanent connections and the successful transition to adulthood for older youth in foster care.

I was in the Project LIFE program as a participant before working as the Youth Development Coordinator. Project LIFE helped me find my voice and made me realize that my voice was valuable.

I consider all the things that happened to me as stepping stones leading to where I am today. I would not be where I am if it wasn't for those experiences. I have come full circle from foster child to a leader in the foster care community.

My twin sister and I entered foster care at age 7. Being abused and in a traumatic situation at home was a horrible experience, and I wouldn't wish it on anyone.

Every day we lived in *fight or flight* mode, just trying to survive. But in my mind, even as a little girl, I felt like the things that were happening to us were supposed to happen. I am not going to say I was okay with it because I knew it was wrong, and I didn't know how to get out of it, but I always thought there was a reason for it happening. This way of thinking was my coping skill, and it helped me get through the challenges I was facing.

We were lucky to live in just a few foster homes. We felt like we had a good social worker who made sure my sister and I were together the whole time in foster care.

We were 14 when our foster mother adopted us. Even so, I still strongly identify with my foster care experience.

I live with my sister now. I often think I would not have made it without her. She is the one consistent thing in my life. Knowing that I have a twin that I can share experiences with has been so helpful in my process of growth. I sometimes feel alone, but having my twin helps me know I can get through anything.

Super hard to trust people

Some people think I should be angry with my biological mom, but I'm not. I didn't know her, and we were never emotionally connected. I also don't think about having a dad because I never had one. I think that made it super hard to trust people. At times,

I felt like I didn't have the ability to connect to people, but over time, I have gotten able to trust people a little more.

I hesitate to tell my story sometimes because of how other people may perceive it, but I am getting better at saying this is my story, and I can tell it the way I remember it.

In my early teen years, I looked for role models I could look up to and feel connected to. One of my favorite things to do as a teen was going to the YMCA. I loved going to the YMCA every day to hang out with my peers and to help on projects we would work on while being there. I adored the teen center counselors. I looked up to them. I thought they were cool, and they saw my sister and me in a positive light.

That was a great feeling because I would often feel like there is no one rooting for me. Deep down inside, I knew that wasn't true, but these were the negative thoughts I had in my head.

When the people I connected to would move away or change jobs, I would be crushed because I would feel like I didn't have anyone to look up to anymore. I learned to build up walls and push people away. I would get attached to a person who cared and that I looked up to as a role model, and then they would be gone.

Fortunately, one of the counselors from the YMCA saw value in my sister and me. We called him our Big Bro. We are still in contact today. By chance, from just showing up at the Teen Center as a teenager, I created a family.

I don't exactly know how I began to develop a group of people in my corner. I can say it happened organically. I didn't really think about it because I was always hesitant to meet new people and would push people away a lot. Normally, the people who were super persistent to the point of annoying me were really hard on me and wanted me to succeed; those were the people I didn't want in my life at first.

But at the same time, they were the ones who stuck around and proved to me that they cared.

Today, these are the people who I value the most in my life. As I have gotten older, I have learned to let my wall down. The people I let in are the ones who keep on trying no matter how hard I push back. At one point in my life, I wouldn't even give people a chance, so I had to learn to intentionally break that barrier for myself because I can't make connections if I have walls up.

My Independent Living Coordinator in the Project LIFE Program asked me if I wanted a mentor. My first reaction was no. What was the point? They would be around for a while and then leave.

When are you going away?

He convinced me to meet her with, what else? Food. We met at a Greek restaurant. My mentor and I connected well even though I was already planning my exit strategy. I was certain she wouldn't be around for long. Several months into the mentoring match, I asked her straight up, "When are you going away?"

She wanted to know why I asked her that, and I told her people don't really stick around that long, or if they do stay, they may try to harm me in some way. She said she would stick around as long as I wanted her to.

We've been matched for six years. She has been my cheerleader from day one. She's at almost everything I do, and that is so cool. I know I did things that would push her away, but she didn't go anywhere. She just stood there and stayed consistent.

School was always a safe place for me. I love to learn, even though it was very challenging because I learn differently. I struggled in school and needed extra support, but I still love to learn, and I just needed a little more support to reach my goals.

I knew about college, but I didn't know how to apply or how to apply for scholarships. I also didn't think I was good enough for college and doubted myself a lot. I decided to start at a community college first because I heard that you didn't have to take tests to get in, so that is where I started.

It was really hard to navigate in the beginning, but then I got into a program called Great Expectations. They help youth and young adults from the foster care system with academic support, filling out financial aid packets, and other skills that go along with adulting.

It was helpful for me to be around other students who had similar experiences and to have my own advisor. I had barely gotten out of high school, and I wasn't the strongest student in some of my community college classes at first, but I worked hard, and once I got accepted at VCU, I never looked back.

When I was in the Great Expectations Program at my community college, they paid for my tuition and books. For my entire academic career, I have had a job while going to school, and this is still the case today, going to school part-time and working as much as I can to make sure my bills are paid.

There was a time when people would talk about their future, and I couldn't see mine. I couldn't see past a certain point, but I have this drive to keep pushing no matter how hard it gets. I just try my hardest and give my all in everything I do.

I believe we all have different experiences that are challenging. It doesn't mean you cannot reach whatever goal you want. Anything is accessible as long as you're willing to put in the work. Sometimes, you have to work twice or even triple hard to get what you want, but in the end, it is going to be worth it.

It's such a surreal feeling because you spend your whole life talking about something and thinking you can't accomplish it, and then when you do, it is really great.

Another thing that has kept me going is my support network. I always want to give credit to them because without them I wouldn't have made it this far. In Project LIFE, we talk about the importance of permanent connections. You can teach people life skills and communication skills, but if they don't have that one person who is going to be there and help with life challenges, then all that other stuff doesn't matter.

I did not set out to have a support network at first, and I was nervous about letting people in. Not just letting people in, but also allowing people to help me. It was also helping myself and letting my guard down just enough to see if it was okay to allow people in. Once I felt like it was okay, I could come out a little from behind the wall I put up. It takes a long time to get over that habit, but the more I am able to trust people, the habit begins to fade away.

Once you get the hang of sensing who is going to be caring and consistent, nonjudgmental, and positive, then you can recognize that these people are in your life for a reason.

I have some goals. The first is to finish grad school. Then it goes back to that future thing and looking ahead to what's in store for me. I haven't thought that far, but there are some things I am passionate about that I would like to do.

I want to see more provisions for foster youth at the university level not just in community colleges. I also want to use my voice to advocate for increased mental health awareness and changes regarding mental health stigma.

As a result of my childhood, I have my own mental health experiences and have come to accept it and learned to navigate through my experiences. Everyone has their challenges, and this is mine.

I can't change how my brain works, even though I am a person who will try very hard to tackle every obstacle in my path. I have learned to give myself a little more grace and go back to my support network that understands what I am going through.

Mental health means that you can't see it

What if someone had a broken leg, they wouldn't tell you to just deal with it? Mental health means that you can't see it. It's not anything bad. I'm learning how to cope through counseling and support groups at school. Just being around other people with challenges helps me feel not so alone.

One of the cool things I do is lead a group called Youth MOVE, which stands for Motivating Others through Voices of Experience. It is a youth-led, activities-based group, and we work on things to change the stigma of mental health and other things, and promote the power of youth voice! The youth give me so much energy and life. I have fun working with them every month!

At school, I've learned a lot about how trauma affects the brain, and now so much makes sense. I thought something was wrong with me, but school has opened my eyes to understanding my own experiences better. I'm also becoming more accepting of my experiences and being okay with saying no to things that are not beneficial for me and my journey.

Even though sometimes I feel alone, I know I'm not.

I can't tell you how many times that theme has played out. A year before I graduated, I said I wanted a surprise party. One of my friends said *Sophia, how are you going to have a surprise party if you're asking for a surprise party?* I thought that was funny, and I just smiled.

Graduation was a big eye-opener. Everyone came together and put it on. They got all of my favorite things; Chick-Fil-A, a Sugar Shack cake, and other things. I loved it because that meant to me that I exist as a person. They care enough about me to know my interests, my favorite color, where I like to eat. Maybe that's what unconditional love feels like.

That moment made me realize that I have so much love and support in my corner that I should never feel alone. But you know, mental health works in mysterious ways, but I am growing and learning that I don't have to feel that way.

I am very outspoken, which is sometimes frowned upon. When I was younger, I may have seemed disrespectful at times trying to get my voice heard. Today, I use my voice, the skills I have learned, and the strength to inspire youth going through the foster system. I want them to be comfortable with their experience and also to feel valued.

I'm passionate about youth voice and helping youths learn how to advocate for themselves and to speak up in appropriate ways. I want to make sure they feel valued no matter what their situation is and remind them they can do whatever they want to do if they put their minds to it.

I know this because I walked the walk. I still walk the walk.

I went to school. I graduated. You can do this too. No matter what barriers are in front of you, no matter what people's expectations are, you are the driver of your own life, and you got this!

Sophia Booker is enrolled in the Master of Social Work graduate program at Virginia Commonwealth University in Richmond, Virginia while she works as Youth Development Coordinator for Project LIFE. At her 2018 undergraduate graduation from VCU, she was awarded the Black History in the Making Award, the BSW Student Field Impact Award, and the School of Social Work Service and Leadership Award. Appointed by Virginia Governor Terry McAuliffe, she currently serves on the State Executive Council for Student Services. As a two-year research assistant to the Dean of the Social Work Department, Sophia earned a 4.0 GPA both semesters of her senior year. She is enormously proud of her twin sister who graduated from VCU as well, with a degree in Biology.

Tylar Larsen
Your Parents Do Not Define You

I am home on winter break from college, spending time with my family in Poquoson, Virginia while I share my story with you.

I wasn't always from Poquoson. I grew up in Utah, but that seems like a very long time ago.

My life has taken many twists, but I think it's on a straighter path now. Let me go back a bit and fill you in, and then we'll go from there.

So, I grew up in Utah with two brothers. When I was nine, my dad died but I continued to live with my mom. My mom didn't handle things very well and eventually started using drugs heavily. She was in and out of jail, becoming abusive and neglectful.

Child protective services stepped in my freshman year of high school because my mom went to jail and my stepdad left us. We were sent to live with my grandparents for two weeks, but then my mom got out and we were returned to her.

My mother and I clashed constantly, so at the end of my freshman year of high school, I fought her to let me leave. This is how I came to live with my aunt in Virginia. It was also the beginning of the life changing relationship I will tell you about later.

After a year living with my aunt though, I had to go back home to Utah. My aunt was like my mother and the situation with her had become unmanageable. My aunt and my mom had grown up in abusive homes and weren't motherly material.

I was not the easiest teenager either.

I returned to Utah and lived there my junior year. It wasn't long before my mom went back to jail. My stepdad said we could live with him, but not after I turned eighteen because then he wouldn't get government checks for me anymore. He wasn't willing to care for me without financial support. My older brother had moved away, but my younger brother got to stay with my stepdad.

I needed someone I trusted

Since I turned eighteen at the start of my senior year, I didn't know what to do. I was not capable of living on my own yet. I didn't have a job or a place to live. I reached out to the one person who made me feel worthy. The one person who cared for me as a human being. The one person I still trusted.

My most memorable and impactful experience my sophomore year of high school in Virginia was attending Young Life and meeting my counselor and mentor, Lauren. She was a college student at James Madison University (JMU) and worked with high school students in the area where I attended school.

It's really incredible. Lauren had wanted to adopt me when I was fifteen and struggling to live with my aunt, but I wouldn't let it happen. I just thought I was too much for anyone, so I ended up going back to Utah.

I always stayed in touch with her and kept that bond from a distance. Lauren loved me literally like nobody else. I've never felt loved and cared for in my entire life; by my parents or by my grandparents. It was always just dragging along, doing whatever was best for them, but Lauren was so intentional and caring about how I was feeling and what I was going through. We created this bond, and it carried out through a year of living across the country.

I felt like I could really count on this girl and she was not going anywhere.

Saying goodbye to Utah

I was lost in Utah with no direction or hope, so I reached out to Lauren, and she encouraged me to return to Virginia. I left everything in Utah and moved back. I sold everything I owned except what I could fit in my backpack. I said goodbye only to my brothers (because I knew it would be harder if I told anyone else I was leaving). I bought a one-way airline ticket and showed up at Lauren's door. She took me in. It was incredible.

She was twenty-four, and she took me in.

We lived in Chesapeake and I finished my senior year. She and her family wanted to adopt me, but I wouldn't let them. I did not ever want to put that pressure on anybody else.

I knew I was very broken, and I couldn't anticipate what that could be like for somebody else to take me in.

It was like the whole situation was just too much. I definitely felt like I was a burden. At least my mom convinced me that I was difficult.

So, I felt like *if she doesn't like me, you're not going to like me. My parents couldn't love me, so how are you supposed to love me?*

I finished high school and I didn't believe I stood a chance of attending college. I had changed schools every single year of high school, and it affected my education. I probably should not have graduated.

Fighting for my education

I actually had to fight the school board to attend my senior year because there were no legal documents of Lauren being my legal guardian. My mom could have called and filed a complaint against me as a runaway at any moment. Anyway, I didn't do well in high school, so I didn't believe there was a way that I could get into college.

Lauren really pushed me on this. Since I completed high school as an independent student, my college application fees were all waved. Lauren encouraged and helped me to apply to about twenty schools and I think I got into eleven of them.

I didn't want to go to any of them.

I did not have any idea of what I would study or what I wanted to do with my life. How could I choose a school? However, I loved Harrisonburg when I lived with my aunt, so therefore I loved JMU, but I didn't get into JMU.

Lauren had gone to JMU and suggested the nearby community college, but I didn't want to attend a community college. Lauren convinced me that the stigma of community college was ridiculous, and she said she could help me get into a Young Life house near JMU. It felt so of the Lord, I had to do it.

Now I live in a Young Life house and attend Blue Ridge Community College. I'm still not doing great in school, but I'm working on it.

Choosing my passion

Last Spring, I started a business and now I'm the business owner of Tylar Brooke Photography. It began with me hating college and feeling like maybe I needed an artistic outlet. I pulled out my old camera from high school and just started taking senior pictures of my housemates. It has blown up from there. I went to visit friends and grandparents in Utah last summer with my camera and ended up doing a lot of shoots out there, and it has exploded. I have booked seven weddings for this summer already.

It's wonderful!

Reflecting on everything, I now know your parents do not define you or who you can be. There are two routes you can choose from, you can be everything that they are, or you can choose to be the opposite of them. It's all about your decisions and what you make of yourself. You can dwell on it and sit in sorrow playing the victim, or you can change who you are and be everything that they weren't.

Somebody will love you.

Family does not have to be your blood family.

Don't feed into the lie that if your parents don't love you, nobody will.

It's not at all the truth. It's a learning process like taking care of yourself and understanding that you do deserve to be loved and learning to love yourself. It's a learning process, and I'll probably continue to learn it for the rest of my life.

I was fortunate to experience a community of help and love through Lauren, her parents, her parent's friends, and Young Life. I know this is exactly where I need to be, and this is where I want to be. Lauren and her family are now my family. My holidays and breaks are spent in Poquoson with the family I chose and who chose me. I feel so loved.

Tylar stepped away from college because her photography bookings demanded her full-time focus. She now operates a successful traveling wedding photography business. She uses her life experiences to guide and mentor high schoolers as a Young Life leader. Tylar splits her time between her homes in Harrisonburg, Virginia and Poquoson, Virginia.

Mike Hill

Making and Repairing
Trusted Connections

'm Mike Hill from Richmond, Virginia. I've spent my life trying to make and repair trusted, healthy connections. I know it's
these connections that have shaped who I am. Some connections have been better than others, but they have shaped me into
an optimistic, empathetic person. It's probably what has driven
me to enter nursing school at Virginia Commonwealth University
(VCU) to pursue a career which focuses on caring for others.

My mother was a fourteen-year-old girl in the foster care system when she had me; she has a total of five kids. I was three when

I was put in foster care with my biological sister who was one at the time.

We have been fortunate to have grown up our entire lives together. We entered foster care together when my mom lost us. She was around sixteen or seventeen, I guess trying to be big and bad herself, dealing with her own issues in foster care.

We went into foster care because she wasn't stable at all. She was young and kind of rebellious and trying to find herself. From what I can remember, we went and stayed with our godmother briefly before we were put into the system.

Luckily for me, I only went to two foster homes.

I went to one home for a few weeks, and that didn't work out. My sister did not go with me, it was just me. My second home was with my parents I have now. My mom had just finished up the whole process of becoming a foster parent, and said she just wanted a little boy. So, they told her, well, we have a little boy, he's three, but he has a sister who's one.

Would she be okay with taking the both of them?

She said, "yes." She ultimately wanted to adopt a boy and a girl and realized she would not have to go through the process twice by adopting the two of us. So luckily for us, that was our final home. My parents ended up adopting us in 2004. We entered foster care in 1999, and they officially adopted us in 2004.

I have a large family if you look at all the children my biological parents have produced as well as the son my adoptive father brought to our family. I have three other siblings from my mom; two sisters and a brother who all still live with her.

My dad has more kids too; four boys and a daughter who's older than me. I have tried throughout the years to have relationships with them. My adoptive parents went through a period where they tried to give my mother a chance to get herself together. She was kind of realigning herself, getting herself back together.

I started going on visits, which I didn't like because of physical things that happened with her boyfriend, whom she later married. I didn't like going and I say luckily, but it wasn't luckily, I think we did that for a month before they got into a very huge fight on my pickup day to go back to my parents' house.

They got into a really bad altercation just before the social worker was coming to pick me up. The police were called, and that was the last straw. Because of that altercation, she lost custody permanently, her parental rights were terminated.

We would go through spouts of time where we would get in contact with her and we would talk consistently for maybe a few weeks.

Then somewhere along the line it would fall off and we'd lose contact with her. I went through that cycle for years.

I was trying to let go of my childhood hurt

When I turned eighteen, I reached out to her and I reached out to who I believed was my dad. I took the liberty to reach out to both of my biological parents trying to just tell them about where I was and that I was trying to let go of my childhood hurt and would like to grow a relationship with them. It worked with my dad for a period. I wouldn't say now that it's completely bad, but I guess we just don't talk as often as we once did.

He was upright and upfront and honest with the situation, how things went down, and he was very empathetic about the situation. My mother on the other hand, not so much. There wasn't a reason to excuse how everything went and she has never to this day fully grasped that things happened the way they did because of the decisions and choices that she made.

My sister is now about the age I was when I wanted to reach out to them. She doesn't know anything else besides the parents we have because she was so young. She knows now that they are not her parents, but in her eyes, those are her only parents. She has no attachment whatsoever to her biological parents. She doesn't care to know, doesn't want to know, she's accepted it. But my adoptive mom always tried to at least make sure we knew who our parents were.

My other two sisters who grew up with my biological mother have reached out to us.

The youngest sister is in a place right now, she's about seventeen, trying to understand it all.

She's trying to understand why we didn't grow up with them, why she didn't grow up with us. She's very upset and angry about it all.

I've answered as much as I can answer, but the questions are not for me to answer. I know I need to at least make an effort because I would like to know how they're doing and what they're doing. If I can help them with anything, I would want to do that because I know how they're feeling.

How different would her life have been if she had grown up as I did, or if we had all grown up together in my biological mother's care? There is a randomness to the directions of our lives that I can't explain or correct for her.

As bad as it was, I'm grateful that I did go through what I have gone through because it made me want to be a better parent.

To be loving and patient, and just to strive to be a better person.

Not that they are totally bad people, but I got tired of trying because I also found myself in a place where if I didn't reach out or say anything, no one said anything to me.

At the end of the day, you had a kid and you have a kid now who is trying to communicate with you, trying to establish some form of relationship with you in which you can easily accessibly talk with them, get to know them. I didn't want to keep chipping away at myself trying to nudge you and nudge you, and nudge you saying, *hey, I'm here!*

There was nothing I could do to change the lack of engagement, so I chose to step back and seek other healthier relationships.

My relationship with my girlfriend has helped me tremendously. She is an amazing, smart, caring person. We have a child together, and I've learned how I don't want to parent from my fathers.

My biological dad was certainly no role model, and while I knew that my adoptive dad loved us, he had his own struggles. He struggled with alcohol and was largely emotionally absent if not just plain absent, clearly a lesson on how not to parent.

But then you can only speculate what it is you're supposed to do and how you're supposed to be. I really take heed to my girlfriend's father, who in my eyes, is a standup, right man, who is pretty cool, a pretty cool dad that I strive to be that same kind of dad. He raised two cool kids, so I now have an example of what I would like to be like. But I keep in mind the road I choose to travel, and the things I don't want to do, because of what I have experienced with my dads.

I am a strong believer in God. I'm rooted in that, and I think that has made this a lot easier for me. My adoptive parents were very loving. They provided a really loving environment for us, a very supportive environment for us. They have always had our best interests at heart.

They were always reassuring my siblings and me of the things that we could do. They never let us get down or wallow, and they pushed us to be the best they knew we could be.

We also grew up in church and just having that foundation of faith helped a whole lot.

I've learned other valuable lessons on this journey too.

If you find something that you enjoy where you can lose yourself, you can make it day in and day out. That for me was music. I chose to be involved with chorus from elementary school until the time that I graduated. That was one environment where I could just lose myself if I was having a bad day.

Choose to find something that just makes you happy

I knew that if I just listened to some music or went to chorus, it would change my day. Just being in there, and being with good people, friends and doing something that I loved to do, made a definite change in my day. So, choose to find something that just makes you happy, that you enjoy. It helped me a lot in middle school.

I also learned you need good friends.

Get around some good people, don't be afraid to be around people. Some people who kind of go through foster care already have a jaded perception of people. Don't be afraid to make those good, healthy connections even if it's just one person or two people that you can connect with. You don't have to spill your everything to them, but then just honestly having a cool connection with someone helps a lot. It helps to have someone on your side and in your corner because it makes going through tough times easier.

Because in time with that, if something's wrong, that's one person that's going to say, "Hey, what's going on?" I had a friend like that. He and I are still thick as thieves to this day. I met him in fourth grade. We played little league football together. His dad was a coach, and we became friends from little league and then ended up attending the same middle school.

Trusted connections are important for us all.

Right now, I'm grateful for my girlfriend. I didn't realize until I got into a relationship with her that I had been carrying a lot of the baggage and weight of my issues and childhood emotional trauma on my shoulders. From childhood to this point in my life with her, I had been carrying a heavy load.

We are trying to build a relationship, build a family, and all of that now. I have learned you have to talk about it. It's not always going to be easy, but it gets easier to talk about. So, you've got to find your person or persons. You have to make your connections: with people, with hobbies, and maybe even with something greater than yourself.

Mike is currently a nursing student at Virginia Commonwealth University in Richmond, Virginia. He expects to complete his training in 2020. He also plans to marry his longtime girlfriend in 2020. They hope to make their home in Richmond after their marriage and Mike's graduation.

Pamela Brooks
Claiming My Past

My name is Pamela Brooks, and I was in the foster care system in the state of Illinois through the Department of Child and Family Services. I went to foster care two different times. Here is how I got there.

I was born in Louisiana. There wasn't a lot of stability. I don't remember ever living in the same place two years in a row. By the time I graduated from law school, I had been to eighteen different schools, often transferring mid-year.

My family: mother, father, younger brother, and I, moved a lot. There was some domestic violence between my parents. I also remember the beginnings of my mother's mental illness. Through professional training, I've come to recognize it as an adult. As a child though, I didn't understand what was happening to her.

My earliest memories include happy times. I *remember* a good relationship with my dad and some positives about my mother.

As time went on, however, things got worse. My birth father walked out on us when I was eight years old. I never laid eyes on the man again. Years later I tracked him down. He apologized and said he was sorry. He said he shouldn't have left me and my brother, knowing how my mother was.

After I tracked him down, he visited my younger brother and birth mother (who lived only an hour and a half away from where I was in college), but he never came to see me. I think he was afraid to face me. But at least I got an apology from him and he validated my memories of that time frame. He took his life in 1986, and the opportunity for healing was left unfinished.

My mother had a tendency to take a lot of prescription drugs, drink, and be with men who drank a lot. As I said, we were constantly moving. It was her pattern to leave me, and my younger brother by four years, with strangers so she and her boyfriend at the time could have alone time together.

One of her boyfriends was the youth minister from the Baptist church we attended in Louisiana – he is the one who moved us back to North Carolina. My mother and her boyfriend took jobs working on the Cherokee Indian Reservation at a school for troubled boys. Looking back, it is actually bizarre and also extremely fortunate we were never left with people who either harmed or abused us.

We lived in low-income housing and often in housing projects, but we were fed and had a roof over our head.

An argument

The relationship between my mother and the youth minister became abusive. She was pregnant and fell down a flight of stairs during an argument with the baby's father (the youth minister). Shortly thereafter, we moved to a housing project in Asheville without her boyfriend.

My mother went into labor early and lost the baby she was carrying. We were too poor to afford a burial plot, so a church on the Cherokee Indian Reservation in North Carolina (a church we attended on occasion) donated a burial plot for the baby.

As an adult, I have visited the Cherokee Indian Reservation and found where the baby is buried. Seeing the gravesite as an adult confirmed once again my childhood memories are accurate.

My mother had told me and my brother that she and the youth minister were married, and he had adopted us and changed our names. After they broke up, I learned that they were never married, and we were never adopted.

My new last name in the fourth grade had been a forged name.

After the relationship with the youth minister ended, we were moving around a lot again and she was going from man to man. It was not the kind of lifestyle anyone would want for a child.

At the end of seventh grade, my mother married a man who had a drinking problem. We moved to Illinois. Once again, there was domestic violence, probably the worst I had seen. He went after her and she pulled out a butcher knife and stabbed him in the leg. I think it was self-defense. The police were called.

We never saw that man again.

Books were my friends

Growing up, I knew my biological family on my mother's side. They all thought my mother was a bit crazy, but no one ever stepped in to help us. When I became an adult, these family members acknowledged my mother's problems and their failure to step in. Also, at that time there were no other protective factors for us.

My mother would go from church to church and beg for any assistance they offered. Because she was a church beggar, we were usually in situations where people of faith were around us. Teachers and church people were my only protection. We moved so frequently; I didn't have time to cultivate friends. Books were my friends.

I don't remember exactly how it happened, but in the ninth grade, my mother and I had an altercation. I called child protective services because by that point, I had an awareness that this was not okay.

I was put in foster care, without my brother, in two different homes for two weeks. Because school was my only stability, I insisted that the Department of Child and Family Services place me in a home on the same side of town in which my high school was located, which is why I had two homes in a two-week span.

The goal of foster care is always reunification if possible. I was returned home. My mother was pregnant again by another boyfriend to whom she was not married. She had the baby prematurely. He needed a great deal of special care and guess who was the baby's primary caretaker? I was, what is called today, a parentified child.

I cared for my ten-year-old brother, a sick newborn, and myself. My mother demanded that the house be immaculately cleaned daily by me. I took care of my siblings, went to school, came home and then resumed being the parent in the house. I also had a boyfriend and was really good friends with his mother. The pressure I was under at home led to us breaking up, but I will return to that later.

My next boyfriend's mother worked for the Department of Child and Family Services. It was Christmas time and my mother had always had a thing about Christmas. She had some sad memories around that time of year.

On December 26, 1980, for some reason, she was insistent that I take the Christmas tree down that day. I refused. It is the only time I remember walking out of the house away from her and defying her. I went to see my boyfriend and his mother.

While I was gone, my mother tried to kill herself and the baby. She had blown all the pilot gas lights out. The house was surrounded by fire fighters and the police when I returned home.

That was my breaking point. I said, I'm done. I can't do this anymore. I knew that if I stayed with my birth family I would not survive emotionally, and possibly, physically.

My ten-year-old brother and I went to stay with friends while my mother was in a psychiatric unit. I can't remember where my infant brother went. When my mother got out of the psychiatric unit, she picked up my brothers and left the state.

When we went to court for my foster care case, my mother did not appear and did not fight for me. I don't remember everything about that day, including even if I had a GAL (guardian ad litem), but I do remember exactly what I wore!

They said they could not find my biological father. Frankly, I don't think they looked very hard. That made me think, if I become a lawyer, that is not how I am going to practice law.

Nobody has a perfect life

So, in January 1981, I entered the foster care system for the second time and remained there until my eighteenth birthday. During the time I was in foster care, I had multiple placements. One thing I learned from multiple foster placements is that nobody has a perfect life. My second foster placement was pretty good. I was doing well in school and had a job. I could basically do what I wanted.

One day at the end of my shift microfilming newspaper articles, my foster care worker showed up at my job with all my belongings on the backseat of her car. My foster family didn't want me anymore.

I had gone to work that morning with no knowledge that they didn't want me. I learned that their biological son was jealous of me, so I had to go.

In my next placement, I moved in with an air traffic controller, his wife, and their two-year-old child. This happened the week that PATCO (the air traffic controller labor union) went on strike and President Ronald Reagan fired all the air traffic controllers. We didn't have any real connection. My high school homecoming was that year, and they were not even around to take pictures. I was parenting myself again, so I requested another family.

On February 12, 1982 I moved in with my last foster family. I still have a relationship with my foster mom and foster brother. Unfortunately, my foster sister died recently from cancer.

They offered to adopt me, but those were the days before the Chafee Act. The Chafee Act provides funding for foster kids to go to college.

I didn't have that.

If I was adopted, I would receive less federal money, so I did not accept their offer of adoption. When I turned eighteen, the State of Illinois sent me a letter stating I was emancipated. In hindsight, I made the right decision. I was on my own to pay for college. I used scholarships, Pell grants, and loans.

I headed off to Bradley University without anyone and no real support system. My foster family let me return to their home for a couple of years until it was obvious our lives were going in different directions.

I got married my junior year of college, perhaps because I needed a family. We both earned our degrees, and I began work at a law firm, which led to attending law school at night after spending a full day at work.

After law school, I landed a job as a law clerk in the Circuit Court of Loudoun County. It was a wonderful opportunity. Then I went into private practice. My practice just fell into the Juvenile and Domestic Relations Court, and that is exactly where my heart has always been leading me. I think a lot of that has to do with my background.

For a very long time, I never told anyone in my professional world about my early years. It was something I kept very close to the vest because I always had a sense of shame over where I came from. It doesn't make sense, but I think that's something a lot of foster kids feel. We're not like everybody else.

I understand now that I got married for all the wrong reasons, and we eventually split, but we split on good terms. We have three children.

Remember that first high school sweetheart, the one whose mother I was really good friends with? Well, I married him and adopted his two children. We became the parents of five children!

My brother, the one that was four years younger than me, also ended up in foster care. Our mother had physically abused him.

When I learned of it, I called Child Protective Services. That brother eventually returned to live with our mother (she promised him a car). However, the emotional abuse and manipulation continued, and he left again when he was eighteen. That brother was adopted by his best friend's mother as an adult.

The youngest brother tracked us down years later because he wanted a family. He suffered emotional abuse and will probably carry the scars for the rest of his life.

We all have families now, so life is good, but because of our mother, we each brought some things into adulthood that probably don't make sense to other people. Christmas has always been a trigger for me because December 26 was the last time I was with my biological family. I have learned how to deal with it, but it is a journey.

My mother was an ill woman. As she was dying, I went to see her. I thought it was the right thing to do. I found her still arrogant and controlling. It was hard to believe.

I have been very blessed

I would say I have been very blessed throughout my whole life. Despite all the horrible things that happened to me, there were always good people to guide me on the right path.

I particularly remember a couple of my high school teachers and my foster mom in my last home. There were also what I call the "God people." That's what I called the people my mother left me with when I was young. They saw something in me and encouraged me, not only to aim for college, but also to not repeat the patterns of my birth family. I have tried to do that, but I still carried shame into my adult life.

It was probably 1996. I attended a symposium as guardian ad litem with a juvenile court judge. We were watching a video about foster care. One child was talking about how as a foster kid you kind of live your life out of a Hefty bag because you don't really have any attachments. When I agreed with the child to my colleague, I realized it was the first time I had disclosed to anyone in my professional community where I came from and what my story entailed.

It finally hit me. I had been working hard trying to help kids to not be ashamed of their lives, and now I needed to claim mine. What I realized is living as a foster child is actually something to be proud of. It makes you a stronger person.

Fast forward years later, and I have the opportunity to serve as a juvenile court judge, which I think is the best job ever because I get to engage with foster kids regularly. I let them know that the person who is making decisions for them understands some of what their journey is. I understand what it's like when all your belongings are in a Hefty bag.

So many kids think it's their fault and they carry that innate shame. I want them to know *this is not your fault.*

You are a beautiful soul with value.

You matter.

Who knows what great things you're going to accomplish?

To the young person on a downward spiral, I ask what interests them, "talk to me about those things. Now go pursue that! You have to be you, whether it is fixing things, blue hair, or music. Focus and follow your interests."

Instead of doing this woe is me thing, I say to the kids in front of me, "there is not a single person on this planet who can't point to some tragedy in their life. Everybody has baggage and you have a choice."

You can take that, and you can say, *I'm going to suck on sour lemons and just be angry and upset or you can add a little water and sugar and make lemonade.* I personally prefer lemonade.

If you don't put a positive spin on life and try to pass it forward, why are we here and why are we doing what we're doing? I truly believe, looking back at my whole life story, and I am a

person of faith, that God helped me take all these horrible things
that happened and turn it into something positive.

Sweet lemonade.

    *Pamela Brooks received her undergraduate degree from Bradley
University in Peoria, Illinois followed by her Doctor of Jurisprudence
from George Mason University School of Law in Fairfax, Virginia.
She and her husband have successfully launched five children. In her
free time, Pamela serves as the Umpire in Chief for Little League
Virginia District 16. Pamela umpires both baseball and softball and
has umpired in three Southeast Region Softball Tournaments, having
received her World Series recommendation. Pamela also volunteers at
her church.*

Jimmy Vaughn
We Don't Give Up

At the beginning of my life, I lived with my divorced mother. She was a heavy drug user and I was the result of her infidelity. She had grown up in foster care and I believe drugs were her coping mechanism. I carried the only piece of advice my mom ever gave me throughout foster care.

We were playing baseball and I kept missing the ball. I threw my bat down, and she told me, "You can't just give up. You've got a team; you've got people out there on the field who care about you, and you can't give up on them, and they're not going to give up on you. You're not allowed to give up. We don't give up."

Having that ingrained in me so early on in my life and hearing her words run through my head as background for many years kept me going.

I entered the system at age seven, under temporary managing conservatorship, which means the state is temporarily taking care of me until my mother or a relative is able to do so.

I lived with a man for a year who was supposed to be my dad, but when a court-ordered test proved I was not his child, I was taken to a shelter. That day was absolutely terrifying, and I felt such a deep sense of rejection.

The workers in those places have a really hard job, but most of them were just really good people.

A ray of light

As I saw other kids get adopted, I wondered about me, and the workers would always respond with, "You'll find a home. Just give it some time, you'll find a home," and that stuck with me. It really was a ray of light.

Then one day, a day just like any other day, a CPS worker told me they had found a home for me and today would be my last day there. I grabbed my stuff, and we drove about three hours to a tiny county in Texas, population 120.

The house was a trailer embedded in the ground with a lake in the back. After the social worker left, I got my first warning sign that this was not going to be a good home.

The dad yelled at the brothers for doing something small. From then on, I was scared of him. I started school and wanted to impress the other kids. I struggled at school because I was an outsider and not part of their community yet.

I already understood concepts that were being taught, which created tension between me and the teachers. I stole for sport, not because I was a foster kid, but because I grew up without any sense of boundaries. My mom had let me do whatever I wanted.

Eventually, one of the teachers put me in a group for gifted and talented students. That experience cemented education. I really enjoyed learning. My brain liked it. It was rewarding. But problems were happening at home.

My parents had brought more kids into the house. That's when the beatings started.

They lasted about four years. I dreaded going home. I have a vivid memory of living on the edge every single day. I told adults about it, but I was told to work on my own behavior. In the sixth grade, I complained to my teacher.

The nurse saw the bruises on my chest, and CPS was called. They removed me from that home.

At this point, I remembered what it was like to have a mother who actually loved me. I know she was an addict, but she loved me. I remembered her bundling me up in the winter and keeping me warm when it was really cold outside. When I had an earache, she was right there. I knew that beating your kid was not love. I was leaving this home and getting a new family.

The next home was so different from the first. No one ever explains that children in the foster care system are traumatized and a new home has new rules and you have to learn the rules fast or you're going to spend a lot of time in trouble.

My new home was very structured. I didn't understand the rules and why they were in place which created immediate problems. It was like an internment camp with a strict wake-up time, school, and lots of chores. If the chores were not done perfectly, you were grounded.

For the first three or four months, I was always grounded. We did a lot of hard physical outdoor labor. The mother was always telling me I would *never amount to anything*, but I still had a light on, the light my mom lit when I was a little kid.

I was enrolled in Upward Bound. It is probably the reason I went to college. In the ninth grade, I attended summer Upward Bound Camp for six weeks. It is hard to remake yourself at school, but Upward Bound was such a melting pot of kids from different school districts that I was able to remake myself and meet a lot of new friends.

It was a nurturing environment, both educationally and emotionally. I stopped taking medication and felt a glimmer of hope because I could get along fine without it. I grew a lot at camp and when I got home, it was a big shock because I was back in a prison-like environment not being allowed to mature.

My identity was developing. I had a sense of self and wanted to become a doctor or lawyer. But I wasn't encouraged in this home. I was on the wrestling team at school and often found myself without a ride home after practice. I was resourceful and would figure out ways to get home even if it meant I had to walk.

I was pretty miffed that my foster parents wouldn't let me get my driver's license. The final straw was when they said I hadn't done my chores and wouldn't give me a ride to an Upward Bound retreat. I just lost it and said I was going to run away. Their son, who was a pretty buff dude, tried to stop me physically.

Later when he left the house, I ran away to Upward Bound. The two counselors there called CPS.

I was not going back to that home.

I ended up in a respite home of all girls. It wasn't the right place for me which is understandable. When there is only one guy in the house, the girls can't talk about lady things, so I was placed in a shelter. My wrestling coach knew my situation and found a way to get me placed in his home.

I still talk to him to this day. He was a good parent; it just didn't work out. He didn't have the right training to deal with trauma. He did everything possible to make it easier for me, and that meant so much. I went on wrestling and family trips to Montana, Hawaii, California, and Colorado. There was food in the house, and I could just go in there and get it without asking.

But there were some struggles. I had a hard time following the rules. He was a concerned parent, but I felt the doors squeezing in on me, and I feared it was becoming like the home I had run away from.

One weekend when he was away, I went to stay at Jeff and Cindy's respite home. These parents were amazing. I saw a family for once. Cindy and Jeff are white, and they had two black daughters who they clearly loved. I came from a racist, *podunk* place and to watch them actually love people and their kids was incredible!

I was with them three or four days and had the time of my life. I told them, "I wish you guys would adopt me."

Cindy said I could come over whenever I wanted. She only had to say it once. There was some fighting and gnashing of teeth, but my therapist and CPS worker finally gave in and moved me to Cindy and Jeff's.

Being in a loving, nurturing home gives pain a time to catch up. Your mind starts to realize what you've been through. When you find people that love you for the first time in a long time, it does weird things to you. I finally got to look back at everything that had happened to me and appreciate where I was, but I was also depressed.

I was a junior in high school and I had missed all the sports tryouts and my classes wouldn't count toward graduation. I didn't try and ended up not doing very well in school. Cindy and Jeff were teaching me independence and encouraged me to go out and get a job to start saving for a car.

So I did. I began working full time at a grocery store where I ran into some less than reputable people. One was a drug dealer. I wanted to impress him and one day, we smoked weed in his car. It was a terrifying experience. I was scared out of my mind. I was sent home from work and told Jeff and Cindy what had happened.

I ended up in an outpatient facility. I don't agree with that decision, I was just struggling to adapt. I had never touched any hard drugs. My mom had taught me that lesson early on. She had destroyed her life using drugs. But I went because I knew Cindy and Jeff cared about me and they wanted me to get help.

Back in high school, I missed graduation by one point. I was crushed. I cannot tell you how crushed I was.

Add to that, Cindy and Jeff were leaving the foster care system.

They had not renewed their certification assuming I would graduate on time. I was faced with a choice to go to summer school and then hopefully to community college in the fall, leave the foster care system, or stay in the system a little longer.

I wanted to go to college but still needed to take my SAT's and get a driver's license, so I extended my contract with CPS and moved in with a lady, a lady I didn't think should be in the foster care system. I missed Jeff and Cindy. We had really bonded.

If I'm ever a father, I'd like to be like Jeff. I admire that man. He was so smart and compassionate. He was such a good dad and not being able to stay with them really, really hurt.

I had learned the statistics of foster kids, and they aren't encouraging. Only three percent earn a college degree. Many end up homeless or incarcerated. I didn't want that. I think that was a big driver for me. I didn't want to be like those people in my life that I watched destroy their lives.

I grew up watching TV and saw warriors defend people's rights and put the bad guy away. I saw people do good things that were changing the world. I wanted to be one of those people, more than I wanted to be broken.

I felt like a lot of people in my life had given up on me. When you are the only person in your own corner you just have to play that Rocky theme song and get up and run up those stairs and just train, train, train and do what needs to be done. That's what I did, and that's what I still do.

Every day, I remembered what my mother taught me so long ago. Do not give up!

I finished high school and was ready to move on with my life. My foster mother dropped me at a church where I had volunteered. By the next day, I was nineteen and homeless. I had a gym membership from the money I made in my high school job, so I used the shower there. I went to the church every other day because when I volunteered, I could also eat. And then the most amazing thing happened after so many disappointments.

I found a family, a real family. It may have taken twenty-one years, but I was finally adopted! I've known this family since I was nineteen and they have been with me every step of the way since. When I'm struggling, angry, or sad, I have a mom and dad to call. I've got support, I've got family now.

We sometimes clash, but that's what family does, but they also stick with me and hold on to me. They've seen me go through incredible pain and struggle, and they've been there through it all. Having somebody in your camp really helps. Knowing that they were cheering for me and if I failed, I was not only going to let myself down but let them down too, well, that kept pushing me forward.

I had people that loved me early in life, and that really helped. It might be hard to believe that you are loved when your parents are dealing with mental or physical illness because they aren't able to show you the love you deserve. But if you keep moving forward, you will find that love again.

Parents who hugged me and said they loved me

I've shared my story many times with attorneys and judges in the state of Texas. I have testified to legislators. I tell everyone that connection is the source of success, connection and being loved. I think the first foster parents who hugged me and said they loved me were Cindy and Jeff.

You don't succeed without somebody else believing in you, whether it is the person reading your resume, a teacher, or a coach.

My parents have taught me that love is sticking with somebody when they are hurting; committing to them, encouraging them even when they make mistakes, crying with them and when they're angry, being just as angry as they are for them.

I remember a little girl in my kindergarten class. We were doing a math game and she kept guessing the number five. Finally, when she guessed the number five one last time, she got it right.

She looked at all of us and said, "Just because you get it wrong the first time, doesn't mean it's not going to be right later on."

The words of that little girl and those of my mother fit my story and carried me for a long time. I knew I just had to keep going, never taking no for an answer and putting one foot in front of the other every day, until I found the love I was searching for.

Jimmy Vaughn earned his undergraduate degree in Government with an emphasis in Legal Studies at Texas Woman's University in Denton, Texas. He is currently a law student at Texas Tech University in Lubbock, Texas. He has been a member of his adopted family for ten years, and he wants Texas foster children to know that financial help is available for them to realize their educational dreams. No matter which state you live in, never take no for an answer!

Jade Morris
Rams in the Bushes

My foster care journey began before I even knew myself. My birth mother had a mental illness.

When I was six months old, the landlord found me alone in the apartment. There were no family members to take me in, so neighbors and friends stepped up and cared for me. Everybody loves babies, but I learned from Social Services records that when I got a little older and a little more difficult, perhaps around four or five, I was alternating between my mother and a neighbor's care.

One day my mother didn't pick me up from school, so the principal took me home. That's the first foster home I remember. It was a decent home, but my mother found out where I was and began bothering the parents. I was moved to juvenile hall which housed both offenders and non-offenders.

We slept in crates and ate the same three meals every day. I eventually went back home, but it didn't last long. There were a lot of incidents, but when my mother used me as a human shield to keep from being stabbed, I was permanently removed. I remember going to court. I think I was seven.

I was molested in my new home, but by then I had become one of those children that nobody wants, and I couldn't tell the truth to save my life, so no one listened to me.

It took getting really harmed to be believed. I was moved to what would be one of about five foster homes between that time and sixth grade. I was involved in a fight at school with a teacher and was expelled. My next move would be across the bridge to Oakland, CA. I was raised there and went to another six foster homes. In total, I lived in eighteen foster homes. Each one seemed to be worse than the one before. But…

When you are young, people speak into your life and say things you don't understand at the time, but later you play it back and you think, *oh, that's what that meant.*

In one of my homes, there was a lady living across the street who would always say to me, "There is something that you are destined to do. What you don't want to do is ruin it before you get a chance to do it."

I just thought she was a Crazy Lady and then one day she said, "I've seen a lot of children come and go out of that house, but you're destined to be something and when you make your self-discovery and figure out who you are destined to be, you're going to be so great, you're going to amaze yourself."

At the time, she was just the 'Crazy Lady' to me!

In another home, there was a lady living upstairs. I call the people that spoke into my life, my "rams in the bushes."

If you know the Bible story of Abraham and Isaac, you know what I mean. "Rams in the bushes" were the people who were there for me right when I thought I couldn't do it anymore. They provided the encouragement I needed, exactly when I needed it. The Lady Upstairs was one of my "rams in the bushes."

She was just a real nice lady. She would give me whatever she had; fruit, a sandwich, anything. Then one day she asked me if I had any talents. I said no, "I didn't."

Then she said, "Well then, make sure you get a good education." I'm thinking *I'm not really good at school right now*, but something about that statement as I'm getting ready to start high school, just told me I should try to study and see where it takes me. I had seen enough of poverty and people with problems around me and I compared them to the people on TV. I knew there had to be something better out there.

You could not convince me that this was the only existence. I refused to believe that this is why we are born. I'm also starting to figure out that I want something else, a nice family, a car, not lofty things, just things I can call my own.

Now the Lady Upstairs, do you know what she would do every time she saw me?

She would say, "How are you doing at school?"

There were two tracks at my school, a vocational track and a college track. I asked my counselor for the college track. She looked at my prior grades and put me in the vocational track. I got all A's that semester, and the next semester she honored my request to try the college track.

I didn't do very well because I wasn't prepared. However, in that track, I met an anthropology teacher, Mr. Hamilton. I will never forget him. He asked me what I wanted to do, and I told him, "I want to go to college; I just don't know how to get there."

Fix my attitude

He said if I would fix my attitude (I did have lots of attitude) and if I came to school early every day at 7:30 a.m., he would help me with algebra. So, I did that every day, and I stayed after if I needed more tutoring, and he helped me get through!

The next year, Mr. Hamilton asked me, "Who are you?"

I said, "I don't know."

"Well," he said, "if you don't know, no one else ever will."

Then he said, "Are you determined?"

Again, I said "I don't know."

He said, "I watched you walk four miles to school every day and get here by 7:30 because you needed help. I think that says you are determined."

He told me that if I saw myself as a determined individual, I wouldn't let obstacles get in my way of doing what needed to be done. When I discovered that I had determination in me, I started looking for other things that were in me that I didn't know were there.

That's what started the catapult.

The Lady Upstairs is still asking me how I'm doing in school and I am beginning to feel like she has an expectation that I'll do my best. Before her, my circumstances were so bad, people understood if I couldn't do well. There was no expectation of me, and I had lived up to every bit of that.

Once someone pointed out there was something worthwhile inside me, it switched on a light for me. There was good stuff in me that just got buried underneath all the mess, the abuse, abandonment, molestation. It was like a messy closet, I needed to pull all the mess out and find the cute pair of shoes I needed hiding under all the junk.

I had a new guidance counselor my senior year who said something that pierced me, and I lost my *oomph*, and yet it may be the reason I ended up getting a doctorate. She didn't want to waste precious spaces in accelerated classes on me. She predicted I would end up cleaning hotel rooms. Now when I look back, I see Mr. Hamilton understood how deflated that made me feel, and he spent the whole year making sure I went to class and building me back up from that comment.

So, Mr. Hamilton, The Lady Upstairs, and the Crazy Lady were my "rams in the bushes" that gave me my focus.

It was a rough year because my birth mother came back into my life. It did not go well. That same year, I had worked and saved up over $700 for the prom, grad night, a class ring, my senior pictures and had given it to my foster mother to hold.

I didn't know about banking. When I went to get it, it was not there. The Lady Upstairs found out and bought a prom dress for me. I had no life skills, so she taught me how to shave my legs and under my arms. She paid a beautician to fix my hair. The Lady Upstairs saw I had worked hard, and she just did all those things for me. Surprisingly, my biological mother even paid for my senior pictures.

The Crazy Lady had planted an idea in my head, and Mr. Hamilton had watered it. Now I'm getting ready to be an adult, to age out of the system. The Lady Upstairs asked to be my Godmother! I thought I might be too old, but I agreed and ended up staying with her.

I signed up to work for Kelly Services and then, because I had been in foster care, I applied and was accepted at San Francisco

State University. I was put on academic probation after the first semester and kicked out after the second!

What am I doing? I've got to do something.

I joined the military.

The military was the best decision I ever made because it took me away to see the life that I always knew was possible. I got to meet different types of people from all kinds of backgrounds. I still kept finding "rams in the bushes."

I saw normal families with normal husband and wife relationships. I found out that people went on vacations. Yet, my attitude was still bad. I was so defensive; I didn't want to let anybody in. If someone came too close, it made me nervous. I wanted friends but at the same time I didn't want them. I was on guard about everything.

I had determination and desire, but I was missing some key elements. What I didn't have was discipline and the ability to handle my emotions. Without those key elements, I didn't know how to employ the good in me. The military taught me discipline; how to be organized and structured and how to have a sense of control.

Discipline

You have to have discipline in order to get where you need to go. Once I got that, then I was able to do the other things I wanted to do. I got married, started college and had two children, all while being active duty military and getting deployed.

I was only twenty and shouldn't have gotten married. I had no idea how to be a family or what it even meant to be a wife or a mother. The marriage lasted four years.

The turning point came one day when my first baby (I was pregnant with my second) would not stop crying. Would not. It didn't matter what I did; feed her, change her, hold her. She just wouldn't stop crying. I'm at home, exhausted. I picked her up.

With rage in my mind, my desire was to shake her. In that moment, I looked into her eyes and my whole entire world shifted because I decided history would not repeat itself. It wouldn't. I put her down in her crib, closed the door, went outside and broke down. I don't think I've ever cried that hard.

All I said was, "God I know I haven't talked to you in a long time, but I know you're there. Here's the thing. I have no idea what I'm doing. There's nobody to call because I don't have a family, but I will not let history repeat itself. I'm going to need a little bit of help, because I want to be the best mother I can be, I just don't know what to do."

I sat there a while longer and then went upstairs to get my baby and she just breaks out laughing. I hug her and tell her I will be the best *mother* I can possibly be for her. So, that was my turning point to say, *I don't have to be the generation before or the generation before that. I can change the course. I don't have to be the bad part of what people have told me.*

That's when the Crazy Lady's words ran through my head, "You are destined to do something great," and I decided it starts right here, right now. I decided I was destined to be the greatest mother on earth.

It is only as I look back at moments of discouragement, and the Crazy Lady telling me I am destined to be somebody, and Mr. Hamilton asking me who I was, that I am able to say, *"Oh, now I see."*

I was not always in a position to hear, but the seed was planted. It might not start to grow for years until someone comes along to nurture it, but the time would come when the light would turn on and I would be ready to receive it. Then later I would be able to start planting seeds of my own.

Once I got the tools I needed, I was able to put it all together and trudge through life. Did I have some setbacks?

Yep, sure did.

Was it always easy?

Nope, sure wasn't.

But I kept moving forward and listening when people were trying to impart their wisdom to me. I might learn something from a sixteen-year-old or a sixty-year-old, it didn't matter because different perspectives allow you to see something that you may not be able to see on your own.

We all need each other. I learned to listen even if something didn't make sense at the time. I have been through a lot of seasons in my life as an airman, a mother, a wife, a student, and I know a season will come when it will all make sense and I can use what I have been given by so many "rams in the bushes."

Jade Morris received her Bachelor of Business Administration from Wayland Baptist University in Plainview, Texas after which she earned a Master of Human Relations from University of Oklahoma in Norman, Oklahoma. She wanted to give her daughters an example to follow, so she completed a Doctor of Organizational Leadership with a specialization in Information Systems and Technology online from the University of Phoenix. Jade remarried and has four daughters including one child adopted from the foster care system. She likes to plant seeds and has fostered eight teenagers.

As she says, "I knew I wanted to do foster, because I wanted to do it right." She retired from the Air Force after twenty-one years of active service. Thank you for that, Master Sergeant Morris!

Melvin Roy
Whose Life Am I Going to Touch Today?

March 26, 2015 is the day my life changed forever.

I was in freshman Spanish class working on an assignment when the phone rang. My Spanish teacher at the time, Señora Bey, picked up the phone and immediately turned to me and said that they needed me in the front office.

So, I left the room and walked down to the front office and the entire time I was walking, I was just thinking to myself, *what does Mr. Brown want to talk to me about now?*

Once I entered the office, I saw six social workers staggered around and I couldn't help but wonder what was going on. As I stepped into Mr. Brown's office, I saw my social worker sitting there on the couch, so I sat right next to her.

She asked me how I was doing and proceeded to say this to me: "Based on the three-month investigation and all the evidence we gathered, we have decided to place you and your sisters in foster care."

Now at that moment, I was so shocked that I had to have her repeat herself. Once she said it again, I went upstairs to get my backpack from my class but while doing that, I was holding in all my emotions because I didn't want my class to see me upset.

Once I grabbed my stuff, I asked my teacher if I could use her phone to call my mom. When she asked why, I just told her that it was an emergency. She allowed me to call my mom, so I went into the hallway and immediately broke down trying to tell my mom that they were placing us in the system.

She couldn't understand what I was saying at first because I was so emotional, but once I calmed down a little, she started panicking and then we hung up the phone.

Three months prior to this, I had reported to the school that my home was not a safe place. My two sisters and I were interviewed by Greater Richmond SCAN (Stop Child Abuse Now) which resulted in the three-month investigation, and ultimately our removal that day in March. Removal was not what I had expected.

The next day was surreal

Fast forward a little. My little sisters and I were all placed with a family on the southside of Richmond. Initially we thought that we were not going to be able to stay in our home schools, but they managed to work out transportation for us. I was in high school, and my sisters were in elementary and middle schools. Going back to school the next day was hard because I had to start a new life.

All I had was a new outfit I purchased from Burlington the night before which was a graphic t-shirt, some black joggers, and some black and white sneakers.

I had to go to school and explain to all my teachers that I did not have any of my schoolwork, nor my homework because all my school supplies were at home with my mother, and we were not allowed to return home.

I was forced to immediately start telling everyone what had transpired. If I didn't, then people would've thought that I did not care about my education and assume I was slacking off when in reality, I had no supplies with me so that I could thrive.

Life immediately started getting more difficult not only at school, but at home. My sisters were not adjusting to being in foster care. They missed our mother dearly and displayed it through their interactions with our foster parents.

I, on the other hand, told myself that I was just going to make the best out of it because I already knew it was going to be challenging for these people, especially since we were their first foster care placement. My sisters and I started going to therapy and support groups through United Methodist Family Services (UMFS) on a regular basis so that we could feel more at ease with our situation, but it only made my sisters more tense about everything.

Deciding to stay in foster care

While we were in care, my mom attended parenting classes and received other services put in place for her so my sisters and I could return home. During that time, we were able to have supervised visitations with our mom which put us at ease. After about eight months, my sisters went back home to our mother, but I decided to stay in foster care.

Why?

I felt that my mom and I were never going to have the same relationship because of what happened and her losing her children. I feared she would not be able to forgive me for the initial complaint to the school and our relationship could not recover.

At the same time, I was benefitting from the programs being offered by the UMFS. After I decided to stay in foster care, I committed to engage more in the support groups offered through UMFS and conferences put on by Project LIFE. Through engaging in those supports, I was not only able to find my voice but also find others who were in the same situation as me. I was able to build genuine relationships with other youth in foster care and use my voice for not only my betterment, but the betterment of those around me.

While with the UMFS, I served on a youth advisory board as the Vice President. I facilitated workshops at conferences around the state of Virginia, and I was able to attend meetings with the Children's Bureau in Washington D.C.

However, along with the periods of up, there were also some periods of downs.

I was still struggling in school because although I wanted to stay in foster care, I could not find the balance between my school life and home life.

I was also still dealing with the fact that I decided to stay in foster care, and I would always question myself on whether I had made the right decision.

Due to my inability to find that balance, my GPA dropped severely, and I was about to be removed from my high school. I attended a public college prep high school which was academically challenging. It was at that moment that I realized that I had to get my life together and push through. I realized that the struggles and hardships I was facing were only temporary and that there was life after high school.

A commitment to my future

I made a commitment to myself and my foster parents that I was going to work hard to bring up my GPA and graduate from Richmond Community High School (RCHS). Once I made that commitment, I had my eyes focused on not only graduating high school but to also attending Old Dominion University.

Because I saw that there was hope for myself, I was able to graduate from RCHS, and even though I was at the bottom of my class, I was proud of myself because I made it to the finish line.

Once I transitioned from RCHS to ODU, I was able to flourish. I started an organization on my campus called Foster-U which aims to encourage higher education in foster youth in the surrounding communities through community service, mentorship, and workshops. I started the organization because I saw the need for foster youth to attend four-year institutions, and I recognized that there were no programs in Virginia that encourage higher education for foster youth.

I also started this organization because of something my first foster mom would say to me, "Melvin, when you pass, people will not remember the car you drove or the house you lived in. They will remember whose life you touched and what difference you made."

Because of her constantly saying that to me, I now live everyday asking myself, "whose life am I going to touch today?" Due to my passion for helping other youth in foster care, I was invited to participate in the FosterClub internship in Seaside, Oregon.

I flew to Oregon and stayed in a house with ten other interns from different states. During that time, we learned how to become better advocates for youth in the foster care system and how to create youth advocates who can advocate for their peers.

During my time there, I traveled to Montana for a youth summit where we conducted workshops with foster youth and taught them needed life skills while also engaging in meaningful discussions about their futures. I also traveled to Camp to Belong in Oregon, which is a camp that is focused on Sibling Reunification.

During that week, I was able to witness youth who had been separated from their loved ones, reunified with them, and engaged in fun activities with them. It was truly a life changing experience. By doing that internship, I was able to see another side of life, as well as another side of Melvin that I never knew was there. Because of the internship, I now have dedicated myself to creating champions in other adults so that they can create champions in other youth who will in turn inspire champions in their peers.

I can say the only way from here is up!

Melvin is a Richmond, Virginia native currently studying at Old Dominion University in Norfolk, Virginia where he majors in Human Services with a minor in Psychology. During his time in college, Melvin has been very involved on and off campus. He has founded an organization called Foster-U which seeks to encourage higher education for foster youth through community service, mentorship, and workshops. He has also interned with FosterClub in 2019 where he spent seven weeks traveling the country to impact foster youth across the United States. Melvin also is the president of SPEAKOUT, the youth advisory board for Virginia which aims to improve the lives of the state's foster youth community. Melvin has a long-term goal of furthering his education at George Washington University in Washington, D.C. to one day become a U.S. Senator on Capitol Hill.

Dijonia Hines
Becoming a Strong, Solid Mother

I am Dijonia (DeeDee) Hines, and I ended up in foster care because my mother and I did not have a good relationship growing up. She drank a lot and was a single mom raising five kids. That's not really an excuse for some of the things I went through, but now that I'm older and a single mom too, I understand a bit more.

I felt different than my brothers and sisters. I never felt like I belonged in their family at all. I was the Dorito in a can of Pringles. I loved them, but I kept my distance.

My father was not around to give my mom the love she needed, so she had different guys moving in with us. I was raped by her boyfriend when I was nine years old.

When I told my mom what happened, she didn't believe me. To hear that from the person who is supposed to protect you the most, made me feel nasty, abandoned, unloved, and ugly. I had to live in the same house with him for two, almost three years until, for her own reasons, she decided he wasn't the one for her. I blamed myself and my mother really distanced herself from me.

I didn't know at the time, but now I know I was depressed. I went looking for something that would ease the pain I was feeling. I was only ten, but my body didn't look ten. I met a twenty-four-year-old man named Spade who said he loved me and made me feel pretty. Basically, he told me everything I wanted to hear.

My mom had failed me, and I had no dad to fall back on and so at the most vulnerable point of my life, I was like, *okay, he is that one.* When I turned eleven, he asked if I was ready to be a grown woman. I felt like I owed him because he got me out of my deepest, darkest feeling. He made me feel on top of the world. That was when he started prostituting me.

He rewarded me with things I had never had in exchange for doing things I knew I wasn't supposed to be doing, but it felt right because he had proven to me he loved me. At twelve, I was pregnant. My mother never knew.

We don't do babies

People just seemed to think I was just getting bigger. I didn't even know I was pregnant until the day I started contracting. I had a little boy that I wasn't able to see or hold or keep. After that day, I never saw him again. My pimp said, "No, we don't do babies." I was devastated. By the end of the week, I was prostituting again, and then serious physical abuse started.

If you were to talk to my mother now about my elementary and middle school years, she would say they were terrible. Nobody understood where I was coming from. Nobody understood the anger I had inside me and why I was so mean. Everyone said I was a problem child, and my mother's favorite line was that I just wanted attention.

I looked for peace anywhere I could find it.

Sometimes I would go home and just relax, cry, and talk to myself. I gravitated toward writing because it was a way for me to get jumbled thoughts out of my head. It worked for a while until it didn't, because writing can't cure everything. I started cutting my arms, to just feel pain and to snap me back from my thoughts.

I felt betrayed by mom and dad and this guy who I thought I loved. I was getting suspended from school all the time. It was just terrible. Everyone was so scared of me. My mother got me evaluated so many times, and they just said there was nothing wrong with me. Child and Family Services entered our family when I was fifteen. I stole from a store and got caught.

Now that the police were in our business, my mom was drinking less but we were fighting, literally fist fighting a lot. The police knew me by name and honestly when they would come, I would be ready to leave. I'd already have the laces out of my shoes. I didn't want to be there anyway.

If living in a jail cell overnight is going to give me some peace, then that was fine. I felt more safe staying in a jail than with my mother. There was no love there. The older I had gotten, the angrier I had become that my mother had not protected me. I had nobody. To this day, I have love for her, and I would never say goodbye forever.

One thing I will give her is that she was there. My dad never was.

She wanted to fill the void left by my father, just like I wanted to fill that void. I understood why she drank.

She got tired of coming to get me from jail. She was so mad and upset to the point where she finally just said, "I don't want her."

CFS came and tried calling around to different family members, but everyone said *no*. They didn't want me. I was a problem child. Then they called my dad. I will never forget that day.

He said he would be there to get me in about two hours. After waiting four hours, they called him back and he said he had decided against it. He had just gotten a job and he didn't want me to ruin his life. That day I ended up going to a foster home.

I chose not to communicate with anyone there. I went into a really bad depression. It was so bad; they connected me with Hillcrest, a child and family center for mental health services. It was pretty cool, but I didn't really want to do it. To this day, I don't feel like any therapist can tell me how to get over my pain if they haven't been through what I had been through.

If you have never been raped, you can't tell me how to get over being raped. No one knows how hard it is, and no one knows how much it sticks to you. Therapists can tell you what science says will work to get rid of pain, but they didn't go through what I went through. It is not one size fits all. I hated going to therapy, so I stayed quiet to the point that they sent me to the Psychiatric Institute of Washington.

For a few days, I didn't eat or talk to anybody, but then I started getting myself together. What made me want to do that was wanting to help the other girls. I had always thought I was the only one dealing with things like this. I was so young. I didn't have the knowledge to understand that it was not just me. There were other girls out there going through the same thing or worse, who were not as intelligent as I was.

Realizing that I was more powerful than them made me want to be their voice and advocate for them. That's what started changing me around. When I got to the point where I was ready to leave PIW, everybody cried; the other girls, the doctors, everybody! They wished me good luck.

After leaving, I had a clearer mind. I had learned a lot about myself. I began taking medicine for anxiety and depression. I went back to foster care with a different family, and I decided to give them a chance. I began talking, eating, meeting with my social worker, everything I was supposed to do.

I was assigned a caseworker, Ms. Stacy McGann. I will never forget her. She is really intelligent, and she helped mold me into the woman I am today. She took her time with me. She didn't press herself on me like the other workers had done. I kept what I had been through to myself for a really long time. I thought since my mom didn't believe me, why would anyone else?

But Ms. Stacy went out of her way for me. She was really calm with me. I got a 4.0 GPA in the ninth grade and was on the honor roll. I was one of those popular geeks. You could talk to me at lunch or recess, but don't bother me when I'm doing my work. I had started turning my behavior around in high school and controlling my anger. I participated in student government and was elected president for the tenth grade, but then I got pregnant.

At sixteen, I moved into an independent living program called Bright Futures. I lived there for a few months but lost the baby through miscarriage which dropped me back down to square one. I was in a deep depression, and I didn't think I could live up to everyone's expectations.

Kids don't understand mental illness. They just think you're not normal. I didn't want to feel that way, so I didn't tell anybody, and I dropped out of school.

My caseworker told me about a military program where I could start pursuing my GED. It was a six-month program, miles and miles away from anything. Coming from a situation where I was locked down by a guy and losing my child and the miscarriage, then being locked down in this military program, just made me feel like I'd been kidnapped.

There was a procedure to walk, a procedure to talk, a procedure to eat. I was not used to this kind of structure. It depressed me to the point where I began cutting my arms. They were like, you're gone, and they discharged me. But those three months had really helped me learn to be humble. People above me had taught me good life skills that I really needed. My mom and I had started communicating more. She had sent me letters and gifts while I was there. Her being there for me made me think she was trying.

I knew our relationship was better at a distance, so when I was discharged, I moved into a new foster home.

When I was eighteen, I could start doing things on my own. I could do whatever I wanted to do for me. I didn't always have to wait for a social worker to sign off on things. I pursued my GED a whole lot more. I took three tests in one day. I didn't pass the math test, which discouraged me, but I did begin to open up and be more vocal with what had happened in my life. I started to accept that that was my life, but it wasn't going to be my future.

Street knowledge

I also accepted the fact that maybe my life experiences had helped me a little bit. When you go through experiences that change your life around, it gives you knowledge. I have street knowledge. I have book knowledge that I learned on my own. I became humbler. I became stronger. I know how to deal with different situations and read people's faces.

I will never excuse what happened to me, but I feel those life experiences helped mold me. I won't ever stop thinking about how my life might have been if my mom had believed me, but would I be the same strong woman I am now if she had?

Would I have my son now if she had?

At nineteen, I was given a CASA (Court Appointed Special Advocate). I was frustrated and had stopped going to court hearings because no one was taking what I said into consideration, and I felt like they were just going to do what they wanted to do. I didn't really want to get in a relationship with her because when I first went into foster care, I went through five or six social workers building a relationship with each one, really getting to like them, and then they would leave.

To get a new person and start the whole trust process all over again, I didn't want to do that. She was going to leave anyway, but she just kept blowing my phone up. So, we finally met. She got to work on everything right away. She was the piece we needed to get everyone in place. I was moved into another foster home that would work for me because at this time, I was engaged and pregnant.

I went to Job Corps, got a learner's permit to drive and finished my GED! I wore a cap and gown and walked across the stage to get my diploma at graduation. My baby's daddy was there to support me.

Eventually, I had to let my baby's father go. It was hard, but I want my son to know that his mom worked hard to give him something solid. I won't take a shortcut. It doesn't give you anything solid, it only gives you an easy way out.

You have to actually go through all the necessary steps to get what you want in life. You have to hit every obstacle, but you will learn from them and you will know how to be stronger. You will know that next time you run into a challenge; you will overcome it.

Dijonia (DeeDee) Hines is a paid intern at CASA DC and a hostess at a local restaurant. Her pride and joy is her son D'Angelo who will always know that she is there for him. She sees her mother every day and has a good relationship with D'Angelo's father's family. She has started a mentor program to shelter teen women.

DeeDee writes poetry and has an event planning, hair and make-up service.

Dijonia Hines refuses to be defeated. She is looking more toward God and letting Him do what He wants in her life. Through her son, He allowed her to birth herself over again.

William Napper

I Didn't Know I Was a Foster Child

My name is William Thomas Napper, Jr.

I am one of eight children.

I entered the foster care system at the age of eight while in the second grade. As far as I know, I was taken into foster care because my mother and father had an abusive relationship.

My mother was also an alcoholic. Of course, I didn't know that at the time. I was too young. My sister and I went to live with Mrs. Nancy Christian. There were other children there; two foster sisters and a foster brother. I was raised entirely by my foster mother and her daughter.

It is interesting to understand, the word "foster" never appeared in my vocabulary until I became an adult. As a child, I did not know I was a foster child.

Segregation was a bigger problem for me than foster care

My other siblings were divided among two other families. We were able to visit together over the years. However, in the 1950's and 60's, we did not have access to public transportation because of segregation. I did not get to see my siblings as much as I would have liked. In many ways, for me, segregation was a bigger problem than foster care.

I remember bits and pieces from living with my mother and father. Once I got to my foster home, I didn't dwell on being in a different place. I just didn't think about it. I had my two biological sisters and my foster siblings. I didn't know anything different other than my foster home. It was just home.

One big thing was we didn't have the communication that children have today. I didn't see people on television having things that I didn't have. The community was similar in that effect. Of course, there were shortcomings. We didn't have the money to do things such as go to the dentist. Since it was during segregation, we didn't have a lot of things to do recreationally. But that was for all the Black kids that lived in my neighborhood, not just foster kids.

I do not think of my early foster years as difficult. I do remember that I moved into a neighborhood where you had to prove yourself to the other kids. After that everything was okay. As the youngest in my foster family, I was kind of spoiled. I was taken under the wings of the older children. Later, a younger sibling came to live with us. People in the Black community looked out for each other. If someone died, a neighbor would raise their child. It wasn't unusual for other kids, not just me, to live in different situations.

The whole community was your family.

I had a lot of consistency growing up as I remained with the same foster family and the same caseworker from age eight all the way through college. I was able to attend college by earning an academic scholarship. I was also given $39 a month by the Welfare Department to attend college. On January 31, 1968, after college graduation, I was commissioned a 2nd Lieutenant in the U.S. Army. My foster mother, sisters, and caseworker were all there.

A one room elementary school

Backing up, I went to a one room elementary school (Chatsworth) that had grades one through five taught by one teacher. I went to Chatsworth through fourth grade. The county built Henrico Central for Black students' where I completed my elementary years. Then I went to Virginia Randolph High School, thirty-five miles from my house. That meant I traveled seventy miles every day.

When I look at the difficulties of the early years, segregation was a bigger problem than being in a foster home. When you put the two together, foster care and segregation, some would think I was disadvantaged, but to me I was not. I was lucky. I was blessed that I had a foster mother who made sure I had all the things I needed. But understand, while we did not have a whole lot of money, we did have land with large gardens, pigs, and chickens. We raised fifty to seventy chickens a year. We never lacked for food. I learned how to take care of a lot of things other than myself.

I recall one of the few ways I was treated differently as a foster child, was having to say my name when I went through the lunch line to get my free lunch. After a while, I stopped saying my name because they got to know me. I was happy about that.

Several things helped me cope as a child.

I always liked to read. I was outgoing and a good athlete. I used all of those things to my advantage. Only two students from my elementary class of twenty-five (Henrico Central) went to college. I feel blessed because a lot of the kids in my class had a mother and a father, but I was the one who went off to college. I received my undergraduate degree from Virginia State University, a master's degree from Hampton University, and did post graduate work at Temple University.

My teachers and the community figured out before I did that I should go to college. Most of the adults in my community had not gone to college. However, they were looking for kids from the next generation who could extend their education. They didn't care if you were in foster care or what kind of family you came from, they just wanted to push the next generation to higher learning.

I was blessed that church members and teachers looked to me as the one they wanted to encourage to go to college. My seventh-grade teacher picked out the exact two people he thought would make it. He was correct.

All my teachers had different roles in my life. Some protected me. I had a coach who pushed and pushed me. Because I was small, he taught me how to compete against taller players. When I began to grow, I got better and better.

I tried out for basketball in college, but a track coach there saw that I had other talents and encouraged me to try out for track and field. Two years later I was competing against the world record holder in the high jump.

After my initial tour of active duty, I became a teacher and head basketball coach for ten years. I stayed in the Army Reserves while teaching and eventually went back into active duty for eighteen years and retired at the rank of Colonel. After which, I returned to education as an Assistant Principal for ten years before retiring.

As I look back on my foster care experience, I don't think it was traumatic. However, as an adult, I realized some of the things I missed out on. I didn't have visits from grandparents. I didn't have cousins, aunts, uncles, birthday parties, the normal things kids have. My mother died when she was forty-four. I did not get to spend much time with her. As an adult, I did have an on and off relationship with my biological father who died at age fifty-five. They both died young.

Things I missed

When I hear people talk about things they did with their parents, I cannot engage in those conversations. I knew I had none of those experiences. That is when I began to think about the things I missed as a foster child. But truthfully, I didn't realize what I was missing as a child. To fill in that gap of not having biological family experiences, upon retirement, I spent twelve years researching my family roots. I traced my family all the way back to 1743. I learned that my family was enslaved by George Washington, the first President of the United States.

I did not know my grandfather or grandmother on my father's side, but as a result of my research, I was able to find many, many branches of the Napper family. I learned that most of my family history occurred about ten miles from where I went to high school.

I learned some of the basketball players I played against in high school were actually my cousins. One hundred people attended the first Napper family reunion. I am reaping the benefit now of having a biological family that I did not have as a child.

My foster care experience put me where I am today. I owe everything I have accomplished to my foster mother. I try to give back because I know kids today are not experiencing the same type of foster care that I experienced. My experience was really not that bad. Since then I've seen some experiences much worse than mine. I understand the goal of the courts today is to return children to their parents. I don't believe that is always the best thing for the child. Sometimes being in a loving, supportive household is better. That is what happened to me. Long term foster care without requiring adoption should always be considered as an option.

Far worse than foster care

I absolutely have positive memories of growing up in foster care and negative memories of segregation. As I said, there are things far worse than foster care. I was a pretty good athlete in high school. I thought I led the state in rebounds. As I was listening to a game on the radio of this white guy that I had always wanted to play against, the announcer said that he led the state in rebounding. I went to my coach and asked him how he could lead the state in rebounding when I averaged more than he did.

My coach said, "Well, yours didn't count."

Because of racism, only white player's statistics counted.

Early on, as an athlete, all I wanted to do was compete against the best. I was denied that opportunity in high school. Several years later, my college coach and the coach at the University of Richmond decided they were going to integrate athletics in the state of Virginia. It happened my sophomore year. In my case, I wanted to make it clear that I was better than my white competition. But relying on how I was raised by my foster mother, I remembered that the important thing was to compete against the best, regardless of color.

We all have a skill

I have some advice for the older kids in foster care today.

You didn't pick your parents.

Nothing you can do about that.

You've got a life to live. So, you can either sit back and complain, or you can move forward. I know it is easier said than done. That is why mentors, especially teachers, are extremely important in the lives of foster children. I had those mentors and teachers when I was in foster care.

The best thing you can do is go to school and get an education. Find out what skill you are good at and pursue that skill no matter what it is. We all have a skill. I wanted to be a college basketball player, but I'm six feet tall and most basketball players are a lot taller. I could have been a hard head and not listened to anyone else, but instead I heard what my track coach said. He thought I could be a high jumper, so I decided to give it a try. Listen to your teachers and other adults. If they see something in you, don't be afraid to give it a try. You never know what may happen.

William really does give back to his community! He is on the Board of Directors of WAFECO (Williamsburg Area for Education and Community Outreach) whose goal is to provide college scholarships for Black males and partner with other organizations to provide aid to under-served families in the Williamsburg, Virginia area. He serves as a Court Appointed Special Advocate (CASA) for abused and neglected children, and he sits on the Virginia State University Alumni Association Board.

He and his wife Sandra Irving Napper both grew up in the welfare system. They each participate with their respective Greek organizations, Alpha Kappa Alpha and Omega Psi Phi, to aid local families in need. They have two children, four grandchildren, and one great grandchild.

William does not distinguish between his foster and biological families. He maintains a close relationship with them all and is looking forward to the next Napper Family reunion.

Asein Ta

From Monastery to Refugee Camp to Group Home

I was born and raised in Burma.

Today it is called Myanmar.

I grew up in a very rural area. My house was made of wood and bamboo. In my childhood, I joined a Buddhist monastery. It was a very common thing in my culture for parents to take their son to the monks and say, "I want my son to stay here and learn about life and go to school." Then they say good-bye and that is it. I was about ten when my dad passed away. My mom's health was not good. She had a lot of work to do raising kids all by herself.

She passed away about four years after my dad. I think I was fourteen. Years and ages are difficult for me to remember.

Before my mom passed away, she asked me if I would be interested in joining a monastery in another country. I said I would, and one day a man, well known in our town, came by with a few other kids, and we started the walk toward Thailand.

We walked all day from our village to the bottom of a mountain, where we slept in a temple. The next day we started climbing the mountain.

WOW! We were climbing, climbing, climbing. Very tiring. Sometimes there was a path, sometimes no path. By the time we reach the peak of the mountain, I just remember how beautiful the sight was.

The wind was blowing, and the sun was setting. It was awesome.

I could see Thailand

On the other side of the mountain, I could see Thailand. Thailand is a more developed country than Burma. They have electricity. We could see all the lights. It was so beautiful. We were excited walking down the mountain.

I learned going down a mountain is hard. You can't lose your grip and slip. It was a dangerous path and getting dark. My legs hurt.

We rested in a Buddhist Temple, and at nighttime, we took a boat and crossed a river into Thailand. There was a guard, who asked some questions. I think we got through the checkpoint pretty easy because we were with the monks and it was late.

We got in a car and some drivers took us somewhere. We were looking all this beautiful high tower building with electricity light.

We were so amazed. We had never seen this before…but that is not where we are going to stay.

We keep driving, driving, driving.

Out of nowhere we stop and start walking by some smaller houses. The next thing I remember, we were in a refugee camp. It was the most houses I had ever seen in my life.

From the Buddhist Temple in the camp, I was on a hill looking down. The houses looked like tiny mushrooms everywhere, on the side of the mountain, on the top of the mountain, in the valley, everywhere!

I don't want to get in trouble

Okay, this is not the beautiful, lighted city. The houses were made of bamboo, more like treehouses on the ground.

The monks at the refugee camp were asked to take care of us. I started as a monk helper; you know regular dress. Eventually I become a novice monk where I have to shave my head.

I don't remember being worried, maybe because I was already grown up in the monastery. I had started there in my village when I was so young. I know the monastery routine.

We wake up very early and have to collect food. People know they have to provide donations. We come back and eat, and then have to practice the Buddhist book.

We have another meal before noon and then a little break. Then we study again.

We take a break and play a little bit, then shower. We pray at night, and then we go to sleep.

Most monasteries do not have formal school, but in the refugee camp, there is a school just for novice monks. We study the religious book Pali, kind of like a Bible.

Buddhist life is very structured, intense, and strict. It is sometimes very scary for kids. It is not a fun place. You want to be doing something else.

It just wasn't an option. What am I going to do? Run away? Go back to my hometown? I just really didn't have a choice.

I try to keep it positive.

I am one of the kids who do the right thing. I don't want to get in trouble. I see kids struggling and I try to be in the right place at the right time.

The consequences of not making good choices can be very frightening. They use corporal punishment. I was so avoiding that. Of course, it is not possible all the time.

I was good. I helped a lot.

One day, the head monk asked if I want to go to an English country. The refugee camp was overpopulated, and they were trying to take some people out. I said okay, I want to go. I didn't think about it for even two minutes. It sounds exciting.

The day I left was very emotional, the whole monastery came down to the bus stop. When we drove away, it was so hard. A lot of things I can't remember, but the feeling just stays there. All the kids I had known since my childhood were there, and I am leaving for the unknown. I knew I was the lucky one, but I felt empty and scared.

They took me and other people too on a bus and then to an airport. I think we landed in California. We were all split up then.

I got on a smaller plane all by myself and came to Richmond, Virginia. My caseworker was waiting for me. They were happy to see me. I didn't speak English. I speak Karen. I just followed where they were going. She had my picture. How did she do that? I had just gotten here!

They took me to a group home. I stay there a couple of months. I remember my first month in my group home. I did not like it at all. I did not understand the language, the culture, the air smelled wrong, the food was not good. I don't have the language to communicate, but because I grow up in monastery, I hold a lot in. I have self-control. I don't explode. I am patient, I just wait and try to observe.

Other than that, I don't have another option. At this time, I know it is going to end, but it is hard. But what is hard? Is it hard because I perceive it is hard or is the situation truly hard? Is it because of me that the situation is harder than it is supposed to be or is the situation just hard? What do I have to compare it to?

If someone in my position feels really sad, because a lot of unfortunate things happen, they might not have the self-control to hold it in. But be patient. Think about it. What are your options? Be patient. It is not going to be forever.

Keep hoping for positive. Think of your life as a whole big book and then think of just one page. That one page might be hard, but it is not the whole book. There will be better pages. This one page won't last. You will grow out of it and go to another page.

Next, I go to my first foster home. Great couple! They work me hard, and I learned a lot. They both were teachers. They want me to learn English quick.

I knew it was good for me, but it was real, real rough. I learned 100 vocabulary words a week – spelling and definition. I am flipping flash cards every second of my life. Flash cards, flash cards, flash cards!

They were there to help me too. They were not lazy. They prepare work for me. Anywhere we go, I'm flipping flash cards.

Public school was just ending when I got there, so I go to summer school. I ride a bike forty-five minutes every morning to catch a bus to get to another school. When I come home, I have chores already lined up, and then I study. I work really hard.

So many times I feel frustration, *I can't do it, I can't do it.* But I hold it. I didn't explode. I knew it was good for me. The Buddhist training definitely helped. As I learn about education in the Western world, I am not a fan of the Buddhist traditional way, but it did help me at that time.

When school starts in the fall, I was speaking English! My grades, my confidence were good. It all paid off.

I am a big fan of foster care. For me, it is a positive note. It is support. They help. I appreciate it. The fact that they offer me family, that is good. They were supportive and positive.

One—I don't expect a lot from foster care. I appreciate every little thing and two – it was a great experience.

The kind of life I want

I moved to second foster home. She is single mom and counting me, there were ten foster children. Seven were siblings.

We were all focused, straight-forward kids, all from different countries. She worked full-time, but she took us everywhere. We went on family trips. We went to Florida and had season passes to Busch Gardens.

We were exposed to the kind of life I want. She is the best. As we each turned eighteen, we left. I needed some space. I used the little stipend from the foster care program, and I have a part-time job at a restaurant. I rent a little room from a family who used to be foster parents.

I have a room and a key! I was also going to John Tyler for community college. Later, I completed my undergraduate and graduate degrees at Virginia Commonwealth University.

Before I came to English country, the only thing we know of America is what is in the movies, animated movies. I create a vision of what I want for myself from movies and from my foster families.

I went into education because I love it. I always love learning and the atmosphere of a school. I am hoping someday I can help more children, especially children from the Burmese community.

Also, I'm a family guy.

I want to have a family. I want to be that guy, the one who coaches sports to all the kids. I love the American life, the normal American life where I work really hard trying to achieve. I have a regular house, regular job, have kids, play sports, not living paycheck to paycheck, but not big money. A movie on the weekend, we do regular stuff. I want to work hard and get there.

I'm telling you—people help me a lot. I could not do it without the right support. It is really hard. I am positive and people want to help me. Everyone I met along the way; they are just super nice. I keep in touch with those people. They are the people who go the extra mile, the extra steps, the extra hours to help me. That is how I get where I am.

Back in community college, I had a life coach, Vicky. She just understood foster kids. To get a license to teach, you have to do a lot of standardized testing. There was one test I just could not get. It was an English test. It was so hard, and I was limited in my time. I took it so many times and could not pass it.

You have to get a passing score to enter the program. I got tutoring. I did everything I could. I missed by one point. I asked them to reassess my score, but they couldn't find one point.

I actually gave up

The next time I failed the test, I actually gave up. I got in my bed, turned on a movie and gave up. Vicky checked on me and I had to tell her.

She said, "Get in your car and come to my office right now."

I turned off the movie and went to her office.

I was in tears. She made a bunch of phone calls and she sent me to see a great, great person. The DEAN! We sat down and we talk. She gave me permission to conditionally continue the program.

I have no choice. I have to study some more.

Finally, I PASS BY TWO POINTS!

It gave me that boost. I was so happy. It turns out, by seeing the Dean, I was awarded a good scholarship and invited to give a speech at the award ceremony. ALL BECAUSE I DIDN'T PASS!

If I had passed the test, I never would have gotten the scholarship. If I had not gone to Vicky when I was so disappointed, I never would have met the Dean.

Vicky is so good. She is wonderful person with all the foster kids.

I was a person who appreciated and accepted help. I think I am a humble person. I don't demand help. I ask for help politely and then when they place expectations on you, I want to live up to it.

Asein Ta is a fifth-grade teacher in Richmond, Virginia. He also holds a real estate license. On the weekends, Asein likes to go to the movies. He thinks the big screen and surround sound are the best. Now he gets to see American movies that are not just animated cartoons. He loves to shop for his classroom. He says his students are always out of pencils. He knows he is living his dream. His next step will be to buy a home, not too big, just a regular house.

Mr. Ta doesn't forget the many people who helped him along the way and keeps in touch with each of them.

Barbara Evans
A Forever Home

Romans 8:18 says, "For I reckon that the sufferings of this present time are not worthy to be compared with the glory which shall be revealed in us." I have held onto this verse and tried to live with it in my heart since my sixth foster care placement.

I hit my low when I lived in a shelter home for kids. It was a home setting for a bunch of kids who didn't have a foster home yet. While I was there, I felt so unwanted, you know, I felt like I was living there and there was no real home for me.

During that time period, my pastor would pick me up each weekend to go to church, but I would just move through the motions. I don't think I ever paid attention to any of it because of everything that was happening. I was so out of it. My next home, my last foster home, was also a mess. However, I knew by this time that I was going to be moving to Virginia. It took a year, but I knew it was coming.

At the age of six, maybe seven, I had my first encounter with any kind of foster care. My parents and I had moved out of our apartment and into a homeless shelter. It was a shelter for families, so there were other kids to play with, which I liked. However, for safety reasons, the shelter required background checks and drug screenings.

The drug tests

My parents did not pass the drug test, and Child Protective Services (CPS) was called to decide if I should be removed from my parents' care. This would be the first time that CPS came and picked me up and took me to a foster care home.

My first home is kind of all blurry since I was so young. I'm honestly not sure how long I stayed there, but I was eventually moved to another home. This placement was more familiar since it was a childhood friend of my mother. Lucy was also my half-brother's godmother. My half-brother is eighteen years older than me, so he was not around at this point. Anyway, I had known Lucy my whole life. I lived with her in Cooper City, Florida for a while. I started going to school there with her son who was my age. It was really a good experience living there because it was with people I knew, and I felt comfortable and safe.

The rest of my experiences get blurrier. I have technically been in seven different foster care homes. I know there were a few times I went back with my parents and then back to foster care. I would return to my mom and then she would end up in jail and I would go to foster care again. I remember sometimes living with my mom or with Lucy and then spending weekends with my dad.

My parents' relationship was very random. You know, they never got divorced, but they were always separated or back together, or my dad would move out after a fight. At one point I did live with my dad for a short while. Their relationship was back and forth, and they fought a lot. They argued mainly because my dad was an alcoholic and would be very aggressive when he drank. His drinking obviously made things worse.

My parents met in rehab, which isn't an ideal courtship. When my mom became pregnant, the whole family became worried. My mom had a stillbirth prior to having me. So, it took a lot for them to even get pregnant and to deliver me.

I didn't know this growing up, but my dad's brother, Tom, and his wife, Jean, were actively trying to get custody of me as soon as I was born. Of course, they were unsuccessful for many years and living so far away in Virginia made it difficult for them to know what was happening with me in Florida. My parents were never physically abusive to me. They had a hard time taking proper care of me. Alcohol and drugs led to neglect.

The long road to Virginia

The actual hard work of getting me to Virginia to live with my aunt and uncle finally started when I was just turning eleven, maybe ten.

I was living with the pastor of my church when my grandparents, my mom's parents, came to see me. They were trying to convince me to move to Virginia. I was very opposed because I thought I would never get to see my mom again. She had convinced me it was a risk. I, as a child, never wanted that to happen. So, I listened to her, and we refused for a while. Finally, my grandparents came to me and said, either you go willingly, or we just drive you there against your will. I thought that sounded illegal, but I decided to go anyway.

It took about a year for Jean and Tom to go through foster care classes and background checks to make sure they were stable for me to stay with in Virginia. In September of 2012, I finally made the move. Jean had to fly down to get me, and then we flew back together.

Lucy had bought me a suitcase to travel to Virginia. I had always moved from home to home using garbage bags full of my personal items. As I was preparing to move the last time, some of my things were stolen from my new suitcase by another foster in the home. She took items while I was in the process of packing, and I didn't even realize it until I got to Virginia.

My mom never wanted me to go. She was really upset with it, but my dad was glad that I said yes. My dad knew it was better for me. He never elaborated on it, but he just felt I'd have a better life with his brother's family. He actually tried for a few years to convince me to go, but I told him no because I was scared that I would never see him or my mom again.

But as soon as I went, he was glad that I did, even though he was not going to be able to see me as much. I was living in a foster home before I left, so I went for a final visit with my mom and dad, and she was not happy.

Once I had relocated, my mom called frequently.

She was nonstop trying to talk me into coming back. She would say that Tom and Jean were just a temporary foster home for the moment. I talked a little bit less to my dad because they were not together during this time. My mom was always talking to me about making sure that I knew I was coming back, making sure that I tell them that I want to come back, stuff like that.

Learning new skills

I didn't really have a lot of manners when I moved in with the Evans. I lacked basic social skills. I missed the training for simple things like holding my fork the right way, or holding my knife the right way, or eating the right way or chewing the right way, things like that. I never even really had a chance to learn. It was left to Jean and Tom to teach it to me.

I also think people in Florida in general and kids in my schools particularly, were very different than the children at schools here. So, when I moved to Virginia I wanted to buy and wear whatever I wanted. I wanted to buy tutus and suspenders and like all these crazy weird things that in Florida people wore, but people didn't wear here.

The tutu

I remember shopping with Jean and asking for a tutu for school. Jean kindly but firmly said to me, "Barbara, I don't think they wear tutus in school here." I argued with her but she, thankfully, held her ground. I think if I would've worn it, I would've looked crazy at school.

I was also very loud and outspoken. I just said whatever came to mind, and I didn't have polite manners. Jean and Tom had to reteach me and be tough about it because I was tough. I was tough to get through to, I would just kind of brush off whatever they said to me until they really drilled it into me. I had not really been taught much before I moved to Virginia.

Now, when I say tough, Jean and Tom were not mean, but I was stubborn and there were a few times where they had to work to get through to me to understand. Overall, they were just straight love, you know. But there were times where they had to be a little bit tougher for me to understand because I never really had experienced tough love. I'm so grateful now for their guidance and patience with me.

Gaining a family

Having "siblings" was a whole other experience for me. Like I said before, I have a half-brother, but he is more like a cousin since I rarely see him, and he didn't ever really live with me. Actually living with siblings was a different experience.

Tommy and Susie were so nice to me which surprised me because I was a little crazy when I first moved to Virginia, a little different, you know? Initially, they were both away at college, but they were super nice. When they officially moved back home, I was not used to it. I was kind of like, "Oh, they're here every day now and I'm not the only kid anymore." So, it was a little bit weird at first, and I think I was honestly jealous because I was so used to being with just Jean and Tom.

When they moved back into the house, I was excited, but kind of jealous, honestly.

I was also jealous that Susie would get to go out and hang out with her friends when I had to wake up for school the next day. I always wanted to get up and hang out with them because I never really had people to hang out with before. I used to tell Jean, "don't worry, I won't go to school, I'll drop out and I'll work at McDonald's for the rest of my life. Just let me hang out with Susie." It never worked; she made me go to bed.

A taste of the good life

In 2014, Jean and Tom said they wanted to adopt me. They actually had wanted to adopt me for many years, but in 2014, I told them that I wanted them to adopt me, and I told my mom that I wanted them to adopt me. She was super upset, obviously. But by that point, I had grown enough to be able to handle myself. I was able to tell her things and not let her talk me out of them.

Once I came to Virginia and had a little taste of a good life, I realized what was happening to me, and I realized I did not want to go back. I'm never going back. I'm staying right here. I told my mom straight up, "I'm getting adopted." It was hard for her to hear, but I stood my ground.

I think what sealed the deal for me was just realizing how good I had it with Tom and Jean. Life had never been like that for me. I had not had the chance to be a child, so when I moved in with the Evans', I just wanted to play with toys like a child. I think it maybe took me a year to get my toy play out.

But, in addition to toys, I also had a bunch of clothes, shoes, and everything that I had never really had access to before. Not only that, but I had food, a roof at a nice house, puppies, a family that was very loving and caring. I think that all of that was a wakeup call to me.

My last foster home was such a stark difference to my new home.

My foster mother locked the cabinets and restricted food access. My meals during the week were mostly provided by the school. I'd eat breakfast and lunch at school. Dinner was usually old leftover food that was not good. To this day, I can't eat leftovers. She never allowed snacks either. She would ask me if I had a tapeworm because I was always hungry. It wasn't a tapeworm; I was just not getting fed.

Living with Tom and Jean was so different because I could eat whenever I wanted. Initially, I would get up at night and sneak food. The cabinets weren't locked! They would tell me to help myself and eat whatever I wanted. We had fresh food every day. I kept thinking, "why are they being so nice?"

I asked myself, *how could I ever leave this, what would make me want to leave?* I had begun making good friends and felt as though I couldn't leave these friends, this family, all of this is so nice.

Jean and Tom were asking me for a while if I wanted to be adopted and you know, they kind of sat me down and really talked to me seriously about adoption and the choice of staying and being adopted and leaving to return to some other kind of life. I appreciate that they included me in the decision process.

Chill out and trust in people

If I could go back and give myself some advice, I would probably tell myself to chill out. I would tell myself there are good things coming my way. There are people who can do so much for you, if you let them. There are good people in the world and they really want to help you, just let them help you and it's going to be a really great outcome. Nothing bad is going to happen anymore if this works, so stop overthinking everything! I guess I would tell myself that things are going to get better and the people around me have good intentions.

All the worrying and over thinking was for nothing. I kept relationships with both of my parents. My dad passed away in 2014 from lung disease; he was a heavy smoker. I did get to visit with him before he died. Jean and Tom took me and one of my good friends from school down to Florida the month before it happened.

My mom had moved back in with him and had been taking care of him. I was glad that they had come together again. I think that was when my mom became clean. My parents had serious struggles with drugs. They lived together for about two years before he passed. It was sad to see him so frail and sick, but I had the chance to say goodbye and find closure.

I have a lot of faith and hope that my mom is still clean. I could always tell when she was on drugs, I could tell within her voice. When I was with her, I could tell by the way she acted, and I think on the phone I could always tell by her voice. I don't hear it anymore.

She moved away from Florida and has a job and a car now. My boyfriend and I visit her on occasion. So, we do have a lot better relationship now. Sometimes she likes to hit me with a little bit of pity, but I think we better understand each other's boundaries now. We try to show mutual respect, and we communicate better.

I know it's hard for kids in foster care right now. It's hard to have the positive mentality of knowing they can get out of this situation and make it through to something better. They need to know there's a way out and there is a way that it'll get better. Kids are being moved way too much in foster care. They're moved around all the time, and it's hard to think you are wanted and valued when being moved around so much. Foster children need to be reassured they are wanted and it's going to get better.

I rely on my Bible verse, Romans 8:18, to get me through rough times. I've stuck by that ever since I began to understand it. It's so true, the pain that we have now and all of the difficulties, problems, and obstacles that we have now cannot compare to what the plan is for our future. I am a strong believer in God. He has a plan for everything. I hope for good families for all foster children, but I also hope that if they end up aging out of care without a forever family, they are able to create a better life for themselves.

Barbara Evans is in her third year of college studying Nursing. She lives with her boyfriend, Aaron, in Poquoson, Virginia with their dog, Ripley. She holds a CNA and works as a nurses' aid at a local retirement village. Tom, Jean, Tommy, and Susie live nearby. Barbara became an aunt in July 2020 and could not be more excited to share her love with a new family member.

Elizabeth Henry
Healing Through Helping

I was born in Tsurupinsk, a small village in Eastern Ukraine.

My dad was an angry drunk who was killed in an alcohol-related accident when I was one. As a result, my mom turned to alcohol which made things a lot more difficult because she couldn't take care of herself or me.

We moved into another small village with our grandparents, and my mom had a baby, my little sister Tanya. After that my mom was never around, so, at a very young age, I had to step up and take care of my little sister. Then my mom had another baby, Ilona. I was left in the house with my ailing grandparents who were old and couldn't take care of themselves or us. I did my best, but I really didn't know how to care for a baby.

Ilona got sick and passed away at seven months. That was one of the harder moments of my life because I felt like I didn't do a good enough job protecting her. After that, my mom just completely went off the deep end.

I attended Catholic Church with my grandparents. I was not a fan because it wasn't fun for me, all that standing and swaying. But on my own time I would pray to a god I didn't really know, but I knew I wanted to take care of my little sister and I had to do something about the way we were living.

I decided we would run away in search of a new life. I was seven. She was five. Nobody was around to take care of us, so I had to go find help.

I took her by the hand, and we literally got on a bus. I think because we were just two little girls, we snuck through. The bus dropped us at a bus station in a random city. The police came and asked us a lot of questions. They knew about my mom and made a decision to take us to a detention center where kids can stay for a short time, giving their parents a chance to get their life together.

If they don't reclaim their kids, then they go to an actual orphanage. There were a lot of kids there, just like us. My sister and I just tried to make the best of the situation by making friends. We were scared because we didn't know what was going to happen.

We went to public school which was also difficult. The other kids would not be friends with us. They made fun of the orphans and would throw stuff at us like we were just dirt on the street. A lot of the kids skipped school to avoid being bullied.

Tanya was my world. I loved her so much. The next hardest moment in my life was when she was taken away from me. I vividly remember that day because it changed my life forever.

Complete heartbreak

I was called into the office and was told Tanya's biological father was there to take her. He didn't want me because I wasn't his daughter. I struggled with the idea of knowing that she deserves the best and that this would probably be the best for her. I was also struggling with the fact that I didn't want to let her go because she was the only family I had. I remember her leaving, walking away with her dad, and she turned around to wave goodbye at me. She had a huge smile on her face. She was just so, so happy, but all I could feel was complete heartbreak.

At the same time, I knew that was the best I could do for her, so I put a smile on my face and said goodbye.

That was the last time I saw her.

From that moment, it was really, really dark for me. I almost didn't care what was going to happen. After so many heartbreaks, I stopped believing that there was hope. I stopped believing that good things could happen. After about a year, I was transferred to an orphanage in Berdyansk. It is one of the better ones in Ukraine. We had food, our own school, and clothes.

House mothers would spend time with us, but it wasn't enough. The most helpful thing for me was having kids around me who were going through similar situations.

I was able to talk to them about their life and find comfort that I was not alone going through struggles. They are part of life. I appreciated having somebody who could listen to me and understand and sympathize. I started to adjust to life in the orphanage. I participated in choir and ballet and was one of the top students.

I don't know why I was the way that I was, I just really wanted to work hard and succeed. I had this internal drive that I think came from the fact that I didn't want to turn out like my mom. I had this will to do better and I put my energy into my schoolwork. I just did my best at the things I could control.

We all went to Catholic Church every Sunday and I hated it, but I started to develop a relationship with God by myself. I prayed at night and slowly began spending time with Him. I would pray and ask Him to show me hope and to show me what the point of living was. Why am I here? Show me a sign, and that's when Operation Christmas Child came into the picture. It is a small part of Samaritan's Purse where millions of volunteers all over the world fill shoeboxes with toys, hygiene items, and school supplies. It is a tool to share Christian Gospel with kids in the worst parts of the world.

A yoyo

Our whole class was called into a small room and told we were going to receive gifts. This was rare for us and we were very excited. I got mine and ran back into the common room and just ripped it apart. I found crayons, a coloring book, little girl's accessories, school supplies, a Bible in my own language, Russian, and the most exciting thing of all…a yoyo!

I took that yoyo with me everywhere. I had no idea what it was. The instructions were in English.

But I didn't care, it was my own. I was so excited. That yoyo represented hope. It gave me strength to go on another day. It made me realize that good things can happen. I knew that in a way, God answered my prayers. I just couldn't believe some stranger somewhere in the world packed a shoebox just for me. It reminded me of God's unfailing love for his children.

When I turned eleven, I was part of a choir at the orphanage that had the opportunity to travel to the United States as a way to promote adoption. The first week, my friend Yana and I stayed with a family in North Carolina.

The second week, we stayed with the Henry family in Virginia. During that second week, they took us to Walmart to buy some toys to take back with us. On the way to the store I fell asleep in the car, so Mr. Henry stayed in the car to be sure I was okay. He says he heard God say, "She is your daughter." He was like, *no way.* This was crazy for him, but he knew what he had to do. He talked to his wife, who said, *yes, let's do it!*

Before I left, using a translator, they asked me if I wanted to be adopted. Of course, I said yes and was very excited. They started the adoption process which altogether took two years. My dad came to visit me once, and they sent packages every month. That was a really difficult time for me because this family that I didn't know was promising they were going to come get me, and they were going to love me and take care of me, but it was taking such a long time that I was slowly losing hope.

Finally, in May of 2007, they came and adopted me. It was exciting, amazing, and difficult because I had to leave my friends behind. Even though it wasn't the best life, it was the only life I knew, and I was comfortable with it. I was just sad. I had this internal struggle. Why am I getting adopted and leaving my friends behind? Don't they deserve a family too?

I adjusted pretty well in the United States. My parents put me in a small private, Christian middle school that was very welcoming. They spent time with me helping me adjust and learn English. I started playing softball and got involved in sports.

As a little girl in Ukraine, I did not feel anger, just sadness and confusion. When I started experiencing normal public high school things in the United States, I began getting some counseling. Things were just starting to come out. When I first came to the US, my dad and I were very close. I had never had a father figure before, so I liked the idea, but I didn't know how to have the relationship. I was never taught that.

In high school, I started getting my own friends and began pulling away from my dad and rebelling a little bit. I had a boyfriend and was pushing the limits. It wasn't until I started counseling that I realized there was some anger inside of me. I had to work through that anger, as well as depression and suicidal feelings, and come out on the other side.

I had kept everything inside.

In counseling, I unpacked everything, step by step with my counselor and worked through those issues. I realized that it would be better for me to let go and move forward and use this as a tool to help others and do something meaningful.

I was involved in sports. Softball was my favorite. I picked it up really quickly. My dad would practice with me every day. I started playing on the high school team and then a travel team. We were scouted by colleges. Virginia Tech offered me a spot on their team, and I committed to play there at the end of my sophomore year. That was really exciting.

When I was fourteen, I found out that my parents were involved in Operation Christmas Child through a local church. I was at Target with my mom shopping for gifts for the shoebox when a memory suddenly came back to me of receiving one of those shoeboxes. That memory sparked the idea of doing more, giving more, and it just grew from there. I asked my mom if we could pack more boxes, and she said *yes*.

The first year, we packed 100 boxes, the next year, it was 162. When I went off to college, I started Operation Christmas Club at Virginia Tech. With the help of my Virginia Tech teammates, altogether in eight years we have donated over 6,000 boxes as a family. It is a tradition and way for me to heal.

I realized something about myself and that is I heal and get through what I went through, by helping others. It brings me joy and helps me understand that what I went through had a reason, and I am able to use those experiences to impact other lives.

The actual Operation Christmas Child organization noticed that I was doing a lot of volunteering for them, and they asked me to become one of their full circle speakers. I went through training, and then they sent me all over the US to share my story and encourage volunteers. I am a walking testimony of the power of shoeboxes. I still continue to travel and share my testimony.

I took a year off following college graduation traveling for Operation Christmas Child. It was awesome to be part of a group that shares the same passion for giving back and for sharing the Gospel. Today, I am in a graduate public health program at the University of Miami. I brought Operation Christmas Child with me. I was a little afraid about it. I didn't know if it would be well received here, but one of my professors let me share my story in front of my classmates, and in our first year, we packed over fifty boxes. That's pretty exciting.

One of the biggest things I have been able to do is to go to Madagascar with Operation Christmas Child and deliver shoeboxes.

It was an amazing life changing event. I just had a moment. We were delivering boxes to orphans who lived on a mountain. They were dirty and didn't have clothes. There was little food and no education. It was a really, really bad situation. They were so excited to see the shoeboxes. A little girl named Sonya was sitting next to me. At first, she wouldn't open her box.

In her native language, Malagazi, I was able to say to her, *Jesus loves you.* I instantly saw a huge smile on her face. I had gained her trust. She went through everything in her box. Her favorite item was a stuffed gingerbread man. I held it in front of her face and tickled her little cheeks with his fluffy arms. She spread her arms for a big, big hug. At that moment, I realized that the gingerbread man was her version of my yoyo.

It was an eye-opening experience for me to remember how happy I had been and now to see that same happiness on Sonya's face. It is my lifelong dream to be able to share that joy with so many more children and the people around me.

Elizabeth Henry received her Master of Public Health from the University of Miami in Miami, Florida in 2019. She is now a Research Assistant in the Department of Public Health Sciences at UM and a Project Coordinator at Florida Institute for Health Innovation (FIHI). Elizabeth is passionate about serving populations at high risk for poor health outcomes and ensuring equity for vulnerable commu-

nities. In whatever arena she finds herself, her goal is to make sure she makes a difference in someone's life. Elizabeth has always had a heart for serving others. She is grateful that God has allowed her to live out her passion through the field of public health.

In her spare time, Elizabeth enjoys running and is currently training for a half marathon. She has also just adopted a tuxedo cat named Oreo. Oreo likes to spend his time napping, playing with his toys, and hiding Elizabeth's makeup brushes under the bed.

Andrew and Kristin Waters
You Are Safe Here; Creating a Foster Family

A ndrew Waters was born directly into a non-family placement. He has been told that when he was about five weeks
old, his mom received a phone call saying, "We found you
a son."

He was probably seven or eight when his parents told him he
was adopted, and he remembers his response was a simple, *hey, cool.*

Adoption was a very unfamiliar topic to him, but his parents
closed their discussion by saying if he ever wanted to know anything about his biological family, just let them know. Now, forty-five years later he still has no desire to investigate his beginnings.

They are brothers

His parents adopted another child out of foster care. While the two sons describe themselves as polar opposites, tall and not so tall, skinny and not so skinny, with only their non-existent hairline in common; they don't think about the biological aspect of their relationship. They just know they are brothers.

Today, Andrew is married. He and his wife Kristin thought they would have a family the traditional way, but that didn't work out for them, so they applied to be foster parents. Within days of being certified, they got their first call for two brothers who were in foster care, and they were asked to provide respite for a long weekend. It was Halloween which is a huge day in their family.

They dropped everything, met the boys, and then carried on with their family traditions of going to a Halloween party and trick-or-treating. Despite the three-year-old's constant string of profanities, when Andrew and Kristin learned that the brothers' next stop would be to a group home until reunification with their biological mother could be completed, their response was *no, they're going to stay with us until this gets figured out.*

The boy's mom followed the DSS plan and within weeks completed the reunification process with her sons.

Kristin muses, "Despite what people think, not all foster care situations are terrible and not all parents don't fix what's wrong and get their kids back. It's not always terminating a parent's rights. Sometimes they just need time to get their stuff together. We realized early on that we were just a stopping point in their travels, we weren't going to be the end result for these two boys."

To this day, both families have a great relationship with each other.

Then they got the girls.

They had them for two and a half years. It was a domestic violence situation. When the girls tried a re-placement with their biological mom, Kristin was the person the older girl called while scared and hiding in a closet during violent episodes. Andrew and Kristin thought they were moving toward adoption when a set of grandparents came out of the woodwork and petitioned to adopt.

The grandfather died on the day they went to court. Despite that, the step-grandmother was awarded custody and currently lives out-of-state with the girls. Andrew and Kristin needed to take a significant break. Losing the girls was pretty traumatizing. The girls had become their kids. Quietly, they both confirm that they still feel like that.

The Waters have always been willing to take children and sibling sets who are elementary school age and younger. They are both first responders, Andrew with the fire department and Kristin as a 911 dispatch operator. Because of their lifestyle and long hours at work, they felt it would be hard to take a child in middle or high school. They knew they would want to establish a relationship with older children before they would be willing to let them be on their own.

Next, they got a call for two brothers who needed a foster-to-adopt situation. This is exceptionally rare. Normally, you don't know the plan for the kids. You might have them for a week, or you might have them for the rest of their lives. The Waters were ready to figure it out together. Within two hours they were in a conference with the Department of Social Services.

The social worker asked Kristin and Andrew if they wanted to see the boy's pictures. Kristin responded, "If you show me pictures, I know these kids are going to be mine."

Eight months later, they were. They legally adopted Nathan (four) and James (ten). The children had been in foster care for a total of two years. Their parents are incarcerated.

The Waters acknowledge their community of friends, many of whom have fostered, adopted, or are themselves adopted. Even their babysitter is adopted. They know many families that have adopted children from Bulgaria. Some of their friends have special needs children from Bulgaria, China, and their local foster care system.

Their children will always be surrounded by children who share their common start. They feel there is a stigma attached to non-biological children that is not relevant in their community. Kristin says she always knew that she wanted to be a mom but never cared if her kids came from her body. They are her kids – it doesn't matter where they came from. She's sad they experienced such horrible situations, but they are her children and she will do anything for them with or without a biological tie.

When a child comes into their home, Andrew and Kristin try to do something fun. Coincidentally, Halloween celebrations have happened twice. They also feel it important to let the children make some choices.

How do they want to set up their room?

Do the siblings want to stay in the same room or sleep separately?

They want them to know that this is their space and it is a safe place.

The Waters try to tie into issues that have played a part in their foster children's previous care. So, with the kids they have just adopted, starvation and malnutrition were issues. They always make sure the children have input in food choices. When they have kids that have been exposed to domestic violence, as a couple they vow to always be positive in front of them and not argue with one another.

They understand the children don't know them and they don't know when things might erupt. They get them a stuffed animal, lovey, or new baby doll that they can always have with them. It really just depends on what their former situation was and trying to tie into it.

They let children come in at their own pace. Some kids are ready to tell everything when they come into care, and some kids don't ever want to talk about it. Nathan doesn't remember much, but James remembers everything. He has been in therapy since his first foster home, so the need to talk is not as great anymore, but he still has a lot of catching up to do. They are addressing those issues now.

Moving slowly is a family mantra. Some of their foster children were afraid of the dark because things happened to them when it was dark. They chose to sleep with the lights on, but they weren't sleeping well. The children would pull their blankets over their heads as a way of protecting themselves while sleeping. The Waters helped them change slowly.

The first transition was from the overhead lights to a floor lamp. Next was leaving on the hallway light and finally to just a nightlight, letting the children slowly get comfortable at each stage. The process took eight months. It is so hard for traumatized kids to sleep. It's a little thing, but it is moving forward at their pace.

None of this is their fault

They want any child who comes into their home to know they are safe. They can be comfortable, and they can be who they want to be. It's so important to teach them that none of this is their fault. Unfortunately, when you're in the kind of situation that these kids have been in, you lose a lot of your childhood, but they still need that chance to be a kid and have fun.

They need to do kid stuff and not worry about being the parent. The Waters want their kids to know that they take joy in being the parents. It's okay to let the adults take care of them and be responsible for them. They can relax.

Andrew and Kristin let the children call them whatever they choose which is big with the transition especially in a community where they can still be exposed to people who were part of their trauma. They let them deal with it however they want, while assuring them that they are safe. When they run into people from the children's past, the Waters acknowledge that *yes that was a person who you knew from your previous home.*

You are safe to say hi to old teachers and neighbors. They want to show their children ways of coping while being polite and teach them how to exit a situation if they feel unsafe.

The Waters jump right into the discipline arena by setting boundaries and expectations from the beginning. They are vocal about behaviors and consequences. They require their son to write down his behavior and what privilege he lost as a consequence, and then they talk about it. He knows going into the next day that it is his choice to control his behavior, and he knows what his consequence will be if he doesn't.

Younger children have timeout, but for older children, it is all about communication.

Kristin and Andrew respect the goals and aspirations of the children who come into their home. They are already disabled from their trauma, and they don't want them to be disabled in their education. They intend to establish the building blocks necessary for every child in their care, to be functional citizens with the tools to choose, whatever they want to do, not young adults disabled by childhood trauma. They can't change the trauma, but they can fix their education and future.

The Waters want their kids to grasp that a lot of other kids are just like them. They didn't do anything wrong; their first families just didn't work out. They surround them with an environment of people who didn't do anything wrong either. It's just how they came into their family.

They can't fix a child's first family, but they can fix this one. They want the kids who come to them temporarily to know that they are not trying to take them from their family. They are their safe landing space for now. They make them know that they are just following a plan and are going to see how this plan works out. Everyone has to do their part, but in the end, it's going to be safe.

Kristen and Andrew Waters' story has come full circle, but it is not complete. They have embraced what they have been given, and with their two adopted sons, they know this family is not yet done fostering!

Andrew and Kristin Waters live in Yorktown, Virginia where they offer their home for foster placements. Kristin is an Emergency Tele-communicator and Andrew a Fire Captain. They have adopted two sibling sets from foster care creating an amazing family of five children: four boys and one girl. All the children in their care are truly a joy and a blessing, each in their own different and special ways.

The Waters support We Are the Echo, recently created by their close friends. The mission of We Are the Echo is to do the best they can to ensure that every child has a home. They assist with transitions from foster to adoption by providing continued care and support. The Waters highly endorse this organization as one doing God's work to ensure that all His children are provided for and loved.

Call to Action

Where are you now that you have met the brave contributors to *Reshuffled*?

We hope that you are feeling inspired to take the next step, no matter how small, towards a future that is better and more rewarding than you ever believed possible.

This book was initially written for those of you in foster care right now. You are the people to be served with full doses of encouragement. While no one can completely understand your unique circumstances, we want you to know there are people willing to stand beside you, people who have worn shoes similar to yours. They are the contributors to *Reshuffled*. They come as close as anyone in understanding your mindset and offer to you, without judgment, game plans, ideas, and role models to spark your will to get up one more time and plan a future that you choose. We remind you that asking for help is a sign of maturity and may only come after asking over and over. Each narrator had a different experience and coping skill they used to reshuffle their own experience. It might help to know that you are not alone, and if a strategy worked for a foster youth before you, then maybe it will help you too. The contributors to this book offer their unfailing resilience to you as evidence that you too can choose where your journey leads.

Perhaps in your profession, you meet foster children every day, whether as their teacher, GAL, CASA, social worker, or health care provider. If you are one of these people, STOP right now to make a promise to yourself and these children to never give up on them, to understand their baggage is too heavy for their young shoulders, and to help them carry the load for as long as it takes. Think of Sophia's mentor. No matter how hard Sophia pushed her away, certain it was just a matter of time before she grew frustrated and moved on, her mentor did not give up. She stayed. The power of just showing up and not leaving proves more than promises.

To the non-foster care community, thank you for jumping on board and opening your heart to understand the complexities of life in foster care. While foster care is one option for children in crisis, you are another solution. Now that you know that even the simplest of overtures to a youth in foster care make a difference, what can you do? Remember Raeshawn's driver or Jade's neighbors; ordinary people who took an interest in helping someone they certainly didn't understand but offered what they had. Use the examples in *Reshuffled* to extend your hand even if it is just a smile or kind words. You might even make the extravagant leap to foster a child of your own. You are needed. The list of children wanting a home is never exhausted.

The narratives told in *Reshuffled* have happy endings. Each contributor survived a difficult childhood and has used their inner strengths to craft meaningful adult lives. But right at this very moment, foster youth stories are being written with unknown endings. The power is within us all to RESHUFFLE our actions and thoughts to influence positive outcomes, whether as a generous supporter of the foster care system or as a foster child doing the hard work. Let's not leave to chance the cards dealt to our youth. We all play a part in reshuffling.

Share your experience in foster care or learn about becoming active in helping foster children by visiting www.ColonialCASA.org.

Acknowledgments

This project would not be possible without the support and encouragement of Colonial CASA, including the Board of Directors, and especially the Executive Director, Victoria Canady. We also are indebted to our mentor in the publishing world, Bud Ramey. His guidance and connections were instrumental in bringing this project to completion. We would also be remiss if we did not thank Jelani Freeman. He was our initial inspiration back on a chilly winter night when he spoke at the College of William and Mary about his experiences growing up in foster care. We are grateful to Morgan James and David Hancock for believing in our project and sharing their enthusiasm for the literary world. Mary Beth Gibson spent weeks editing with the understanding that the individual voices were important. We are grateful for her attention to detail and generosity. Finally, we thank our essay partners. You are each an inspiration to us, and we think to anyone who takes the time to read your stories.

About the Authors

Tracy Gharbo grew up in Central Ohio and graduated from The Ohio State University with a B.A. in Journalism. She has fond memories of her first writing experiences, including as a staff reporter and photographer for the university's student paper and as a student intern in the athletic department's sports information office. She went on to make a career in advertising and marketing and is currently a marketing manager in the healthcare industry. Tracy's interest in child advocacy stems from a difficult period in her early teens that left her feeling unheard and isolated. She works as a CASA to give children in crisis a voice and a reliable advocate for their needs. She has volunteered since 2017 as a Court Appointed Special Advocate (CASA) in Williamsburg, Virginia, where she resides.

Linda Palmer is a former pub-lic-school teacher and business owner. Trained in educational counseling at the College of William and Mary and the University of Virginia, she has volunteered as a Court Appointed Special Advocate since 2012. She values her experience in court mediation and enjoys writing children's books. Linda resides in Williamsburg, Virginia

A free ebook edition is available with the purchase of this book.

To claim your free ebook edition:

1. Visit MorganJamesBOGO.com
2. Sign your name CLEARLY in the space
3. Complete the form and submit a photo of the entire copyright page
4. You or your friend can download the ebook to your preferred device

Morgan James BOGO™

A **FREE** ebook edition is available for you or a friend with the purchase of this print book.

CLEARLY SIGN YOUR NAME ABOVE

Instructions to claim your free ebook edition:
1. Visit MorganJamesBOGO.com
2. Sign your name CLEARLY in the space above
3. Complete the form and submit a photo of this entire page
4. You or your friend can download the ebook to your preferred device

Print & Digital Together Forever.

Snap a photo

Free ebook

Read anywhere

Printed in the USA
CPSIA information can be obtained
at www.ICGtesting.com
JSHW022324140824
68134JS00019B/1275

9 781631 953118